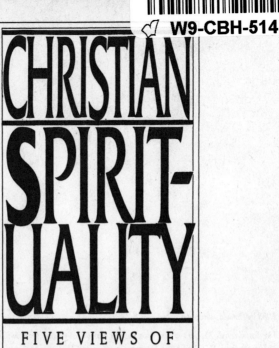

CHRISTIAN SPIRIT- UALITY

FIVE VIEWS OF SANCTIFICATION

edited by
Donald L. Alexander

with contributions by
Sinclair B. Ferguson
Gerhard O. Forde
E. Glenn Hinson
Russell P. Spittler
Laurence W. Wood

INTERVARSITY PRESS
DOWNERS GROVE, ILLINOIS 60515

InterVarsity Press is the book-publishing division of InterVarsity Christian Fellowship, a student movement active on campus at hundreds of universities, colleges and schools of nursing. For information about local and regional activities, write Public Relations Dept., InterVarsity Christian Fellowship, 6400 Schroeder Rd., P.O. Box 7895, Madison, WI 53707-7895.

Distributed in Canada through InterVarsity Press, 860 Denison St., Unit 3, Markham, Ontario L3R 4H1, Canada.

All Scripture quotations, unless otherwise indicated, are from the Holy Bible, New International Version. Copyright © 1973, 1978, International Bible Society. Used by permission of Zondervan Bible Publishers.

Cover photograph by Robert Flescher

ISBN 0-8308-1278-4

Printed in the United States of America

Library of Congress Cataloging-in-Publication Data
Christian spirituality.

   Includes index.
  1. Sanctification—Comparative studies. 2. Holiness—Comparative studies. 3. Spirituality—Comparative studies. I. Alexander, Donald, 1935-
BT765.C4 1988   234'.8   88-29023
ISBN 0-8308-1278-4

17	16	15	14	13	12	11	10	9	8	7	6	5	4	3	2	1
99	98	97	96	95	94	93	92	91	90	89	88					

The Riddle of Sanctification

Donald Alexander

ERNIE STRUGGLES WITH AN HABITUAL PROBLEM OF LUSTFUL thoughts. He has prayed frequently that God would deliver him, but no release has come. Ernie believes that because God cannot look upon sin, God can no longer forgive him. He sincerely desires to live a life pleasing to God, but lacks the personal discipline to achieve his goal.

What should Ernie do? Should he (1) reaffirm the belief that persons stand before God by faith alone, rest in this biblical fact, and simply seek professional help for his personal problem? Or should Ernie (2) seek a special endowment of the Holy Spirit which promises to cleanse the heart from impurity and fill it with divine love? Or should he (3) recall that salvation means that the Holy Spirit has already given him the power to say no to sin, and develop this power to resist by embracing God's law in obedient discipleship—and expect a new response to the world, himself and others to emerge?

The Practical Dilemma

A life of consistent holiness seems unattainable to many believers. Many are discouraged by sin's persistent power to enslave us. Sin often reigns over our lives like sovereign dictator. We want to resist sin's commands, but the strength to do so frequently eludes us. Many believers, therefore, identify with the words of the apostle Paul who cried out, "I do not understand what I do. For what I want to do I do not do, but what I hate I do. . . . As it is, it is no longer I myself who do it, but it is sin living in me. I know that nothing good lives in me, that is, in my sinful nature. For I have the desire to do what is good, but I cannot carry it out. For what I do is not the good I want to do; no, the evil I do not want to do—this I keep on doing" (Rom 7:15-19).

But, after all, no one can live a perfectly holy life—can they? Even the notable theologian John Calvin admitted that "there never existed any work of a godly man which, if examined by God's stern judgment, would not deserve condemnation."[1] How often we have tried to live a life pleasing to God, only to experience failure again and again. Sin rules with such strength that only the coming of Christ himself can abolish its final control. Hence, many believers conclude that the Christian life is a continual moral struggle in which consistent victory over sin will be experienced only in the life to come.

On the other hand, Scripture commands us not to let sin reign in our mortal bodies. But given the power of sin to enslave, this command appears both perplexing and unrealistic. Nevertheless, Scripture clearly presents us with the obligation to live lives worthy of our calling (Eph 4:1). The apostle Peter is one who admonishes the believers: "But just as he who called you is holy, so be holy in all you do; for it is written: 'Be holy, because I am holy' " (1 Pet 1:15-16). The apostle Paul also urges believers to "conduct [themselves] in a manner worthy of the gospel of Christ" (Phil 1:27), and the author of Hebrews exhorts us to "make every effort . . . to be holy; without holiness no one will see the Lord" (Heb 12:14). Surely these biblical commands must be taken literally and seriously. We are called to live lives of moral purity and spiritual integrity.

The practical dilemma is obvious. Sin seems to reign with unconquerable power, and yet we are commanded to put off the old self with its sinful practices (Eph 4:22) and to work out our salvation with fear and trembling (Phil 2:12). But are we being commanded to do something that we are unable to do in actuality? After all, only God can conquer sin and produce holiness in the believer (Heb 9:11—10:10). Furthermore, Scripture declares that the believer stands before God by grace through faith alone and not because of works, no matter how good or moral these works may be. At the judgment seat of Christ there will be no saints, but only sinners saved by grace. Hence the practical dilemma arises: How do we harmonize God's sovereign work in conquering sin with our responsibility to live a life of consistent holiness?

A serious misunderstanding erupts, however, if the practical dilemma is perceived only in negative terms. The biblical message declares that the believer in some real sense has been released from slavery to sin and evil powers (see Gal 4; Rom 6).[2] The continuing struggle against sin, the flesh and the devil cannot minimize the triumph of Christ's death and resurrection. At the cross sinners are set free—free to live! We must keep this liberating dimension of the gospel in mind as we attempt to resolve the tension in our call to practical holiness.

Nevertheless, how to appropriate Christ's victory in the daily struggle against sin remains a practical dilemma for many believers. The active attacks of evil on the believer do not diminish after conversion (see 1 Thess 3:5; 2 Cor 12:7; Rom 16:20; Eph 6:11-12).[3] Indeed, the believer finds the Christian walk fraught with conflict and struggle between desires and actions (Rom 7:18-20). And while there is much difference of opinion on the nature of this Christian struggle, the clear practical tension remains: Believers, on the one hand, do in fact sin; but on the other hand, they are admonished to stop sinning and to walk in holiness and perfection (for instance, see 2 Cor 6:14—7:1; Phil 3:12-14).

Outlining the Alternatives

Attempting to coordinate the tension between God's sovereign work in holiness and the believer's obedient participation is the concern of this book. Each of the five authors of this volume offers a perspective which he believes resolves this tension, and also reflects the biblical message of liberation from the tyranny of sin.

While the reader weighs the authors' views, it is hoped that these essays will inform and assist the reader in comprehending the key issues and eliminate any unfamiliarity with the central doctrinal teachings. Each of the perspectives has been selected because it emphasizes a significant biblical teaching that illuminates the questions in the call to a life of holiness, and because it formulates a logical and systematic view that is historically rooted in one of the main church traditions within Protestantism.

Categorizing the way Christian thinkers resolve the dilemma in the call to personal holiness is a complex matter. Generally speaking, however, three fundamental perspectives or emphases emerge. Gerhard O. Forde (Lutheran) convincingly represents those who stress *faith alone*. Sinclair B. Ferguson (Reformed) and E. Glenn Hinson (Contemplative) present two variations of the point of view that stresses *faith and the believer's responsible participation*. Laurence W. Wood (Wesleyan) and Russell P. Spittler (Pentecostal) offer complementary, though contrasting, views that stress *the unique role of the Holy Spirit*.

Overcoming the power of indwelling sin generally presents the believer with more practical problems than theoretical ones. At the same time, however, what we believe affects how we live. Consequently, it is essential that we grasp the theological underpinnings of the various perspectives represented in this book. From this basis we can realize practical solutions for overcoming sin and living a life of holiness that are congruent with our beliefs.

As you read the five perspectives offered in this book, you may want to formulate a response either to Ernie's situation or to any other that comes to mind, keeping the following questions before you:

☐ What is the foundation upon which the believer may claim and experience victory over sin: faith, a special experience of the Holy Spirit, union with Christ or some combination of these?

☐ How is sin defined: as a conscious, voluntary transgression of the law of God; or as a state of being independent from the sinner's intentions?

☐ How are the "old self" and the "new self" interpreted and related?

☐ What is the function of the law in the life of the believer?

☐ What is the role of the Holy Spirit in our call to practical holiness?

Notes

[1] Calvin *Institutes* 3.14.11.

[2] David Wenham, "The Christian Life: A Life of Tension?" *Pauline Studies*, eds. Donald A. Hagner and Murray J. Harris (Grand Rapids, Mich.: Eerdmans, 1980), p. 81.

[3] Ibid.

The Lutheran View

Gerhard O. Forde

SANCTIFICATION, IF IT IS TO BE SPOKEN OF AS SOMETHING other than justification, is perhaps best defined as the art of getting used to the unconditional justification wrought by the grace of God for Jesus' sake. It is what happens when we are grasped by the fact that God alone justifies. It is being made holy, and as such, it is not our work. It is the work of the Spirit who is called Holy. The fact that it is not our work puts the old Adam/Eve (our old self) to death and calls forth a new being in Christ. It is being saved from the sickness unto death and being called to new life.

In German there is a nice play on words which is hard to reproduce in English. Salvation is *Das Heil*—which gives the sense both of being healed and of being saved. Sanctification is *Die Heiligung*—which would perhaps best be translated as "being salvationed." Sanctification is "being salvationed," the new life arising from the catastrophe suffered by the old upon hearing that God alone saves. It is the pure flower that blossoms in the desert, watered by the unconditional grace of God.

Sanctification is thus simply *the art of getting used to justification*. It is not something added to justification. It is not the final defense against a justification too liberally granted. It *is* the justified life. It is what happens when the old being comes up against the end of its self-justifying and self-gratifying ways, however pious. It is life lived in anticipation of the resurrection.

As such, sanctification is likely not the kind of life that we (old beings!) would wish, much as we might prattle piously about it and protest about how necessary it is. For the most part we make the mistake of equating sanctification with what we might call the moral life. As old beings we get nervous when we hear about justification by grace alone, faith alone, and worry that it will lead to moral laxity. So we say we have to "add" sanctification too, or we have to get on to what is *really* important, living the "sanctified life." And by that we usually mean living morally.

Now, living morally is indeed an important, wise and good thing. There is no need to knock it. But it should not be equated with sanctification, being made holy. The moral life is the business of the old being in this world. The Reformers called it "civil righteousness." Sanctification is the result of the dying of the old and the rising of the new. The moral life is the result of the old being's struggle to climb to the heights of the law. Sanctification has to do with the descent of the new being into humanity, becoming a neighbor, freely, spontaneously, giving of the self in self-forgetful and uncalculating ways. "But when you give to the needy, do not let your left hand know what your right hand is doing, so that your giving may be in secret. Then your Father, who sees what is done in secret, will reward you" (Mt 6:3-4). Sanctification is God's secret, hidden (perhaps especially!) even from the "sanctified." The last thing the sanctified would do would be to talk about it or make claims about achieving it. One would be more likely, with Paul, to talk about one's weaknesses.

No, sanctification is not the kind of thing we would seek. I expect we don't really want it, and perhaps rarely know when it is happening to us. It is the work of the Holy Spirit, the Lord and giver of life. It is given to us in the buffeting about, the sorrows, the joys, the sufferings and the tasks of daily life. As Ernest Becker rightly put it in his classic work (that ought to be read by everyone interested in the question of "salvationing" today) *The Denial of Death,* the hardest thing is not even the death, but the rebirth, because it means that for the first time we shall have to be reborn not as gods but as human beings, shorn of all our defenses, projects and claims.[1] Can flowers bloom in this desert? Can we survive and get used to justification? Can we live as though it were true? That is the question.

The Argument

Talk about sanctification is dangerous. It is too seductive for the old being. What seems to have happened in the tradition is that sanctification has been sharply distinguished from justification, and thus separated out as the part of the "salvationing" we are to do. God alone does the justifying simply by declaring the ungodly to be so, for Jesus' sake. Most everyone is willing to concede that, at least in some fashion. But, of course, then comes the question: what happens next? Must not the justified live properly? Must not justification be safeguarded so it will not be abused? So sanctification enters the picture supposedly to rescue the good ship Salvation from shipwreck on the rocks of Grace Alone. Sanctification, it seems, is *our* part of the bargain. But, of course, once it is looked on that way, we must be careful not to undo God's justifying act in Christ. So sanctification must be absolutely separated from justification. God, it seems, does his part, and then we do ours.

The result of this kind of thinking is generally disastrous. We are driven to make an entirely false distinction between justification and sanctification in order to save the investment the old being has in the moral system. Justification is a kind of obligatory religious preliminary which is rendered largely ineffective while we talk about getting on with the truly "serious" business of becoming "sanctified" according to some moral scheme or other. We become the actors in sanctification. This is entirely false. According to Scripture, God is always the acting subject, even in sanctification. The distinction serves only to leave the old being in control of things under the guise of pious talk.

On the level of human understanding, the problem is we attempt to combine the unconditional grace of God with our notions of continuously existing and acting under the law. In other words, the old being does not come up against its death, but goes on pursuing its projects, perhaps a little more morally or piously, but still on its own. There is no death of the old and thus no hope for a resurrection of the new. The unconditional grace of God is combined with the wrong theological anthropology. That is always disaster. As we shall see a bit later, justification by faith alone demands that we think in terms of the death of the old subject and the resurrection of a new one, not the continuous existence of the old. Unconditional grace calls forth a new being in Christ. But the old being sees such unconditional grace as dangerous and so protects its continuity by "adding sanctification." It seeks to stave off the death involved by becoming "moral."

Sanctification thus becomes merely another part of its self-defense against grace. Justification is rendered more or less harmless. Talk about sanctification can be dangerous in that it misleads and seduces the old being into thinking it is still in control. We may grudgingly admit we cannot justify ourselves, but then we attempt to make up for that by getting serious about sanctification.

Even under the best of conditions, talk about sanctification in any way apart from justification is dangerous. It has a tendency to become a strictly verbal exercise in which one says obligatory things to show one is "serious about it"—but little comes of the discussion. Perhaps one feels sanctified just by talking impressively about it. The result of such talk is what I like to call "the magnificent hot-air balloon syndrome." One talks impressively *about* sanctification, and we all get beguiled by the rhetoric and agree. "Yes, of course, we all ought to do that," and the balloon begins to rise into the religious stratosphere solely on the strength of its own hot air. It is something like bragging about prowess in love and sex. It is mostly hot air and rarely accomplishes anything more for the hearers than arousing anxiety or creating the illusion that they somehow can participate vicariously. We got started in that direction even in the above exercise in this thesis when we talked about how sanctification is "spontaneous," "free," "self-forgetful," "self-giving," "uncalculating" and all those nice things. Dangerous talk. Dangerous because, like love, none of those things can actually be *produced* by us in any way. Theology indeed obligates us to talk about them, to attempt accurate description, but unless we know the dangers and limitations of such descriptions, it leads only to presumption or despair. So let the reader beware!

And so at the very least, we can say that sanctification cannot in any way be separated from justification. It is not merely a logical mistake, but a spiritually devastating one. In fact, the Scriptures rarely, if ever, treat sanctification as a movement distinct from justification. In writing to the Christians at Corinth, for instance, Paul refers to them as "those sanctified in Christ Jesus, called to be saints together with all those who in every place call on the name of our Lord Jesus Christ"; and later, he refers to the God who chooses what is low and despised in the world, even the things that are not, as the source of our life in Christ Jesus, "whom God made our wisdom, our righteousness and sanctification and redemption," so that whoever boasts should boast in the Lord (1 Cor 1:2, 28-31 RSV).

To the Thessalonians Paul writes that they have been chosen by God from the beginning "to be saved through the sanctifying work of the Spirit and through belief in the truth" (2 Thess 2:13). Hebrews says that "we have been sanctified through the offering of the body of Jesus Christ once for all" (Heb 10:10 RSV). Sanctification appears in Scripture to be roughly equivalent to other words for the salvation wrought by God in Christ, a phrase which designates another facet or dimension of sanctification, but never calls it something distinct or logically different from justification. J. K. S. Reid is right when he concludes, "It is tempting for the sake of logical neatness to make a clean division between the two [justification and sanctification] but the temptation must be resisted, if in fact the division is absent from Holy Scripture."[2]

It is difficult to escape the suspicion that the distinction between justification and sanctification is strictly a *dogmatic* one made because people got nervous about what would happen when unconditional grace was preached, especially in Reformation times. Doesn't justification do away with good works? Who will be good if they hear about justification by faith alone? So the anxious questions went. Sanctification was "added" as something distinct in order to save the enterprise from supposed disaster. But dogmatic distinctions don't save us from disaster. More likely than not, they only make matters worse.

Justification by Faith Alone

It becomes clear, then, that we cannot talk about sanctification without first saying something about justification. The difficulty we have arises because justification by faith alone, without the deeds of the law, is a mighty breakup of the ordinary schemes of morality and religion; a mighty attack, we should say, on the theology of the old being. The fact that we are justified before God—the eternal Judge, Creator and Preserver of all life—unconditionally for Jesus' sake and by faith alone, simply shatters the old being's entire system of values and calculations.

As old beings we don't know what to do with an unconditional gift or promise. Virtually our entire existence in this world is shaped, determined and controlled by conditional promises and calculations. We are brought up on conditional promises. We live by them. Our future is determined by them. Conditional promises always have an "if-then" form.[3] *If* you eat your spinach, *then* you get your pudding. *If* you are a good girl, *then* you can go to the movies. *If* you do your schoolwork, *then* you will pass the course. *If* you do your job, *then* you will get your pay. *If* you prove yourself, *then* you will get a promotion. And so on and so on, endlessly until at last we die of it, wondering *if* we had only done this or that differently, perhaps *then*. . . . Though such conditional promises are often burdensome and even oppressive, they are nevertheless enticing and even comforting in their own way because they give life its structure and seem to grant us a measure of control. *If* we fulfill the conditions, *then* we have a claim on what is promised. We have what we call "rights," and we can control our future, at least to a certain extent.

So, as old beings, we hang rather tenaciously onto these conditional promises. As a matter of fact, that is what largely characterizes our *being* in this world as *old*. We hang desperately onto the conditional promises, hoping to control our own destiny. We live "under the law" and cannot get out—because we really don't want to. We prefer to go our own way even up to the last barrier: death. And there we must either hope that the conditionality ends and all account books simply close, or perhaps we make the fatal mistake of thinking that we can extend our control under the conditional promise even into the beyond. We think we have a claim on heaven itself if the proper conditions are met. Religion is most often just the attempt to extend this conditionality into eternity and to gain a certain measure of control even over the eternal itself.

But the saving act of God in Jesus Christ—comprehended in justification by faith alone—is an *unconditional* promise. Unconditional promises have a "because-therefore" form. *Because* Jesus has overcome the world and all enemies by his death and resurrection, *therefore* (and only for that reason) you shall be saved. *Because* Jesus died and rose, *therefore* God here and now declares you just for Jesus' sake (not even for your sake, but for Jesus' sake). *Because* Jesus has borne the sin of the whole world in his body unto death and yet conquered, *therefore* God declares the forgiveness of our sins.

Now, of course, as old beings we have a desperately difficult time with such an unconditional promise. It knocks everything out of kilter. We simply don't know how to cope with it, so we are thrown into confusion. Is it really true? Can one announce it just like that? No strings attached? Don't we have to be more careful about to whom we say such things? It appears wild and dangerous and reckless to us, just as it did to Jesus' contemporaries. The best we can do is to try to draw it back into our conditional understanding—so all the questions and protests come pouring out. But surely we have to do *something,* don't we? Don't we at least have to make our decision to accept? Isn't faith, after all, a condition? Or repentance? Isn't the idea of an unconditional promise terribly dangerous? Who will be good? Won't it lead perhaps to universalism, libertinism, license and sundry disasters? Don't we need to insist on sanctification to prevent the whole from collapsing into cheap grace? Doesn't the Bible follow the declaration of grace with certain exhortations and imperatives? So the protestations go, for the most part designed to reimpose at least a minimal conditionality on the promise.

It is crucial to see that here we have arrived at the decisive point which will entirely determine how we look at what we call sanctification. It is true, you see, that as old beings we simply cannot understand or cope with the unconditional promise of justification pronounced in the name of Jesus. What we don't see is that what the unconditional promise is calling forth is a *new being.* The justification of God promised in Jesus is not an "offer" made to us as old beings; it is our end, our death. We are, quite literally, through as old beings. To use the vernacular, we have "had it." All the questions and protests that we raise are really just the death rattle of the old Adam and Eve who sense that their kingdom is under radical and final attack. No doubt that is why the defense is so desperate, and why it even quite innocently takes such pious and well-meaning forms.

But isn't the unconditional promise dangerous? Of course it is! After all, look what happened to Jesus! It is the death of us one way or another. Either we stick in our conditionality and go to that death which is eternal, or we are put to death to be raised to new and eternal life in the one who lives eternally. The point is that when we come up against the danger and radicality of the unconditional promise, the solution is not to fall back on conditionality but simply to be drawn into the death and resurrection of Jesus. The old being cannot survive the promise, the promise which makes new beings out of nothing. God is the one who calls into being that which is from that which is not. The new being finds its center now not in itself, but in Jesus.

One has only to follow out the argument in Romans to see Paul clearly developing this point. The law, the conditional promise, did not stop sin; it only made it worse. As a matter of fact, the law was given to show sin as sinful beyond measure, a bottomless pit, an endless hall of mirrors. But where sin abounded, grace abounded all the more! But isn't such argument terribly dangerous? Aren't all the careful barriers built against sin suddenly destroyed? Doesn't one come perilously close to saying that sin is somehow presupposed by or even necessary for grace? Couldn't one then justly say, "Well then, shall we not sin the more that grace may abound?" It is a serious question and one that has to be raised. As a matter of fact, if the question isn't raised, one probably hasn't yet grasped the radical *hilaritas,* the joy of grace. No doubt, it is the old being's last question prior to its death. But what is the answer? It does not lie in returning to the law, to conditionality, but rather in the death of the old.

Shall we go on sinning so that grace may increase? By no means! We died to sin; how can we live in it any longer? Or don't you know that all of us who were baptized into Christ Jesus were baptized into his death? We were therefore buried with him through baptism into death in order that, just as Christ was raised from the dead through the glory of the Father, we too may live a new life.

If we have been united with him like this in his death, we will certainly also be united with him in his resurrection. For we know that our old self was crucified with him so that the body of sin might be done away with, that we should no longer be slaves to sin— because anyone who has died has been freed from sin.

Now if we died with Christ, we believe that we will also live with him. For we know that since Christ was raised from the dead, he cannot die again; death no longer has mastery over him. The death he died, he died to sin once for all; but the life he lives, he lives to God.

In the same way, count yourselves dead to sin but alive to God in Christ Jesus. (Rom 6: 1-11)

Actually, all evangelical treatment of sanctification should be little more than comment on this passage. The end to sin is death, not following the law, not moral progress, not even "sanctification" as the old Adam or Eve thinks of it. To sin the more that grace may increase is, of course, absurd and impossible precisely because of the death. To do so would mean to will to return to sin in order to get more grace. That would be like a lover desiring to return to the state of unloving in order to experience falling in love again. Quite impossible! How can one who has died to sin still live in it? The movement is simply irreversible if one catches a glimpse of what the grace is all about.

Furthermore, it is crucial to note that Paul does not tell his readers that they have to get busy now and die. He announces the startling and unconditional fact that we *have* died. It is not a task to be accomplished. All who were baptized into Christ Jesus were baptized into his death, so that out of that death may come newness of life, just like and as sure as the resurrection of Christ. Sin is a slavery from which we escape only through that death. Only one who has died is free from sin. There is no other way. The old self has been crucified so that the sinful body might also be destroyed and we might at last be set free. There is no continuity of the old self to be carried over here. Christ now becomes our life.

Just the sheer and unconditional announcement "You have died!"— the uncompromising insistence that there is nothing to do now, that God has made his last move—just that, and that alone, is what puts the old being to death, precisely because *there is nothing for the old being to do.* The God who says, "I will have mercy on whom I will have mercy," has decided to do just that through the death and resurrection of Jesus. There is no way for the old being to do anything about such grace. The unconditional justification, the grace itself, *slays* the old self and destroys its "body of sin" so as to fashion a new one. It is all over! Christ being raised from the dead will never die again. One can't go back and repeat it. He died to sin once for all, and now he lives to God. Conclusion? You can now only consider yourself dead to sin and alive to

God in Christ Jesus!

So, when we come to the decisive and crucial point about justification and the unconditional promise of grace, it is imperative to see that God is at work making new beings through this (to us) shocking act. The answer to all our questions, to the "death rattle" questions of the old Adam or Eve, lies not in falling back on conditionality, but in learning to cope with death and resurrection. All the questions must therefore be answered with a confident *yes*.

Do you mean to say we don't have to do anything? Yes! Just listen! Do you mean to say that even faith is not a condition, nor is making our decision, nor repentance? Yes! Faith is a gift. It comes by hearing. It is the Spirit's work. It is a being grasped by the unconditional promise, a being caught by the sheer newness and joy of it, a being carried by the Word of Grace. But is not such unconditional promise dangerous? Yes, I suppose it is in this evil age. After all, Jesus got killed for it! But God has apparently decided to take the risk, and sealed it by raising Jesus from the dead. "Wake up, O sleeper, rise from the dead, and Christ will shine on you" (Eph 5:14).

But do you mean to say we can't say *no*? That kind of question is, of course, the trickiest of the old Adam or Eve. But in spite of everything, it must be answered with a confident *yes*—from the point of view of the new being. The old Adam or Eve will, of course, only say *no*, can really only say *no*. The old Adam or Eve wants to remain in control of the matter and so says *no* even while wanting to say *yes*.

So saying *no* is not an option? Perhaps the best answer would be, "What do you want to do that for?" It would be like arriving at the altar for the wedding and answering the big question. "Do you take . . ." with, "Do you mean to say I can't say *no*?" If we see at all what is going on, we would see that even here the answer finally has got to be *yes*: "Yes, I don't see how you can say *no*!" The new being by definition *is* one who says *yes*. One is not *forced* here, one is made new, *saved*—heart, soul, mind. One is *sanctified* in the truth of the unconditional promise of God.

The answer to the persistent questions of the old Adam or Eve is therefore always *yes, yes, yes*, until at last we die of it and begin to whisper, "Amen! So be it Lord!" Sanctification is a matter of being grasped by the unconditional grace of God and having now to live in that light. It is a matter of getting used to justification.

Simultaneously Just and Sinner

But now we must look a bit closer at how the unconditional promise—justification by faith alone—works in our lives if we are to arrive at an appropriate understanding of what we might call sanctification. The first thing to grasp is, of course, that the unconditional promise works quite differently from a conditional one. The unconditional promise, the divine decree of justification, grants everything all at once to the faith it creates. We are simply declared just for Jesus' sake. But that means simultaneously that we are revealed to ourselves as sinners. The sin revealed is not just a misdeed, but it is precisely our lack of faith and trust over against the incredible goodness of God. The sin to be ultimately expelled is our lack of trust, our unbelief. All our impetuous questions are shown for what they are: unbelief, our reservations over against the God of grace, our fear of being made new.

And still we ask, Don't we have to do something? You see, that is all we really planned to do—just a little something! We hadn't counted on being made new! Just that, you see, is the sin exposed! Nevertheless, God simply declares us to be just for Jesus' sake because that is the only thing that will help. That act of God itself finally exposes us as sinners, desperately in need of saving. So then, for the time being, we are, as Martin Luther said, *simul justus et peccator*, simultaneously just and sinner. It is the unconditional grace of God that makes us so. In that, we see the truth. And it is in the truth that we are sanctified. The first step on the way of sanctification is to realize that.

This is radically different from our usual, conditional thinking. Conditional thinking is wedded to the schemes of law and progress characteristic of this age. Sin is understood primarily as misdeed or transgression of such a scheme. "Sanctification" is the business of making progress in cutting down on sin according to the scheme. Holiness or righteousness could not be said to exist *simultaneously* with sin in the same scheme. Righteousness and sin would simply exclude each other. The more righteousness one gains, the less sin there would be. This would be measured by what one does or doesn't do. It would be a matter of works. Grace would then have to be understood as the power to do such works, to achieve such righteousness. The logic would then be that with the help of grace one progressively gains more and more righteousness and thus sins less and less. One strives toward perfection until, theoretically, one would need less and less grace or perhaps finally no more grace at all.

But such conditional schemes pose all sorts of problems for one who wants to think and believe "in the fashion of Scripture," as Luther called it.[4] In the first place, it doesn't fit with the divine act of justification by grace alone, by faith alone. There is no real place for justification in the scheme. If it comes at the beginning of the scheme, it makes the subsequent progress unnecessary. Why work at becoming just if you are already declared to be so? On the other hand, if justification comes at the end of the scheme, it becomes unnecessary. You don't have to be declared just if you have already become so.

The systematic problem is that both justification by faith alone without the deeds of the law and such a scheme of sanctification cannot possibly coexist together. The tradition no doubt recognized this when it insisted on making a sharp and complete distinction between the two, at least in theory. In actual practice, however, one or the other of them generally comes to be regarded as more or less fictional or dispensable. And more likely than not, it will be justification that is so regarded. It comes to be looked upon as a decree contrary to actual fact, a kind of "as if" theology. We are regarded "as if" we were just. Or perhaps it is a kind of "temporary loan" granted until we actually earn our way. Sanctification according to this scheme takes over the center of the stage as the real and practical business of the Christian.

But this leads only to a further, more personal problem in the life of faith if one becomes honest before God. What if the scheme just doesn't seem to work? This is the much celebrated problem of the "anxious conscience" that bothered Martin Luther. What if one is honest enough to see that one is not actually making the kind of progress the scheme proposes? I am told that grace gives the power to improve, to gain righteousness and overcome sin. I am told, furthermore, that grace is absolutely free. But what if I go to church to "get grace" and then get up the next morning and see the same old sinner, perhaps even a little bit worse, staring back at me through the mirror? What then? I am told that grace is free, and that there is nothing wrong with the "delivery system." Not even a bad priest, minister or a faulty church can frustrate or limit the grace of God. But I don't seem to get better. If I am in any way serious, I can only become more and more anxious. I am told that grace gives one the power to love God. But as a matter of fact I only become more and more resentful of a God who sets up such systems and makes such demands. I don't seem to grow in love of God. I begin to hate him! The magnificent hot-air balloon bursts.

Now I face the really desperate question: Whose fault is it if the scheme doesn't work? There are two possibilities. Either I have not properly responded to or cooperated with the free divine grace, or most frightening of all, the God of election who presides over such grace has decided, in my case, not to give it. The scheme leaves me either depending on my own abilities to respond, to remove all obstacles to grace, to "let myself go" and so forth, or it leaves me with the terrors of predestination. Usually, of course, we recoil in horror from the very thought of predestination. We piously wouldn't want to lay the blame on God—and besides, we would then lose all control of the matter!

So all things considered, we would rather take the blame for the breakdown of the scheme on ourselves. If it didn't work, it must be because we didn't do something right. We didn't repent sincerely enough; we didn't really and truly seek him; we didn't wholly give our hearts to Jesus; and so on. But in that case, the more we talk about "free grace" the worse it gets. When the system doesn't work, "grace is free" turns out to mean that there is no way we can put the blame on grace. But then no matter how much we *talk* about the grace of God, absolutely everything then depends on us, on our sincerity, our truthfulness, the depth of our feeling, the wholeheartedness of our confession and so on. The system simply turns against us. While we live as old beings in this age, we simply cannot escape the law.

So it is impossible to put God's unconditional act of justifying sinners for Jesus' sake alone together with our ideas of progress based on conditions. It doesn't work either logically or in the life of faith. That is why Martin Luther came to see that we must take a radically different approach. In place of all ordinary understandings of progress and sanctification, the true Christian life begins when we see the *simultaneity* of sin and righteousness. God begins with us simply by declaring us to be righteous because of Jesus. We begin to see the truth of the situation when we realize that because God had to do that, we must have been at the same time sinners. God would be wasting his breath declaring people to be righteous if they were not actually and wholly sinners! Indeed, as Paul put it, "if righteousness could be gained through the law, Christ died for nothing!" (Gal 2:21).

And there can be no cheating here. Since the declaration of God is total, and depends totally on what Jesus has accomplished for us, the sin simultaneously exposed is total. All the dreams, schemes and pretensions of the old Adam or Eve are unmasked in their totality. Sin, as a total state, can only be fought by faith in the total and unconditionally given righteousness. Anything other than that would lead only to hypocrisy or despair. If there is to be anything like true sanctification, it must begin with these considerations.

If our righteousness depends totally on Jesus, and is appropriated only in the relationship of trust (faith), then we can begin to see that God has two problems with us. The relationship can be broken in two ways. The first would be by our failure, our immorality, our vices. Since we lack faith and hope in God's cause, the relationship is threatened or broken; we go our own way. That problem is usually quite obvious. But the second problem is not so obvious. It is precisely our supposed success, even our "morality," our virtues—the relationship with God is broken to the degree that we think we don't need the unconditional justification, or perhaps even to the degree that we think we are going to use God to achieve our own ideas of sanctity. The relationship is broken precisely because we think it is *our* holiness.

The first problem, our failure and immorality, is usually most easily recognized and generally condemned because it has consequences, both personally and socially. But the second problem, while generally approved in human eyes because it is advantageous and socially useful, is more dangerous before God (*coram deo,* as Luther put it) precisely because it is praised and sought after. It is the kind of hypocrisy Jesus criticized so vehemently in the gospels: "like whitewashed tombs, which look beautiful on the outside but on the inside are full of dead men's bones and everything unclean" (Mt 23:27). No matter how good and useful such virtue is in the world (and we must not fail to see that it *is* really so and does have its place), it *cannot* be counted as sancti-

"Sanctification is part of Just."

fication. Those who blow their own horns when they give alms so as to be seen and admired by the public do indeed have their reward: the praise of others. But that is all they get. True sanctification is God's secret (Mt 6:2-4).

So the first step on the way to sanctification is to see that, before the judgment of God as it comes through the crucified and risen Jesus, we are rendered totally just at the same time as we are exposed totally as sinners. Sanctification is thus included in justification as a total state. True sanctification is at the outset simply to believe that God has taken charge of the matter. Where can there be more holiness than where God is revered and worshiped as the only Holy One? But God is revered as the only Holy One where the sinner, the real and total sinner, stands still and listens to God. There the sinner must realize that his or her ways are at an end. The final assault is under way. There the sinner begins to realize that neither virtue nor vice, morality nor immorality, neither circumcision nor uncircumcision counts for anything before God, but what matters is the new creation (Gal 6:15). Sanctification is not a repair job. God is after something new. He wants his creation back as new as when it came from his hand.

Progress in Sanctification: The Invasion of the New

But is there not such a thing as *growth* in sanctification, progress in the Christian life? No doubt there is a sense in which we can and even should speak in such fashion. But when we do, we must take care, if everything we have been saying up to this point is true. If justification by faith alone rejects all ordinary schemes of progress and renders us simultaneously just and sinners, we have to look at growth and progress in quite a different light.

That brings us back to our thesis: sanctification is the art of getting used to justification. There is a kind of growth and progress, it is to be hoped, but it is growth in grace—a growth in coming to be captivated more and more, if we can so speak, by the totality, the unconditionality of the grace of God. It is a matter of getting used to the fact that if we are to be saved it will have to be by grace *alone*. We should make no mistake about it: sin is to be conquered and expelled. But if we see that sin is the total state of standing against the unconditional grace and goodness of God, if sin is our very incredulity, unbelief, mistrust, our insistence on falling back on our self and maintaining control, then it is only through the total grace of God that *sin* comes under attack, and only through faith in that total grace that sin is defeated. To repeat: sin is not defeated by a repair job, but by dying and being raised *new*.

So it is always as a totality that unconditional grace attacks sin. That is why total sanctification and justification are in essence the same thing. The total sinner comes under the attack of the total gift. That is how the battle begins. How then can we talk about the progress of the battle—the transition, let us call it—from sin to righteousness, old to new?

There are, I believe, two aspects of this transition we need to talk about. The first is that since we always are confronted and given grace as a totality, we find ourselves always starting fresh. As Luther put it, "To progress is always to begin again."[5] In this life, we never quite get over grace, we never entirely grasp it, we never really learn it. It always takes us by surprise. Again and again we have to be conquered and captivated by its totality. The transition will never be completed this side of the grave. The Christian can never presume to be on the glory road, nor to reach a stage, which now forms the basis for the next stage, which can be left behind. The Christian who is grasped by the totality of grace always discovers the miracle anew. One is always at a new beginning. Grace is new everyday. Like the manna in the wilderness, it can never be bottled or stored. Yesterday's grace turns to poison. By the same token, however, the Christian never has an endless process of sanctification to traverse. Since the totality is given, one knows that one *has* arrived. Christ carries the Christian totally.

Looked at from Luther's point of view of "always beginning again," the transition is therefore not a continuous or steady progress of the sort we could recognize. It is rather more like an oscillation between beginning and end in which both are always equally near. The end, the total gift, is constantly and steadily given. But to grasp that we have constantly to begin again—we never can get over it! It is like lovers who just can't get over the miracle of the gift of love and so are constantly saying it over and over again as though it were completely new and previously unheard of! And so it constantly begins again.

The second aspect of the transition of the Christian from old to new, death to life, is that all our ordinary views of progress and growth are turned upside down. It is not that we are somehow moving toward the goal, but rather that the goal is moving closer and closer to us. This corresponds to the eschatological nature of the New Testament message. It is the coming of the kingdom upon us, not our coming closer to or building up the kingdom. That is why it is a growth *in grace,* not a growth in our own virtue or morality. The progress, if one can call it that, is that we are being shaped more and more by the totality of the grace coming to us. The progress is due to the steady invasion of the new. That means that we are being taken more and more off our own hands, more and more away from self, and getting used to the idea of being saved by the grace of God alone. Our sanctification consists merely in being shaped by, or getting used to, justification.

Getting used to justification means that the old Adam or Eve is being put to death, and thus, as Paul put it, "being freed from sin." How might we conceive of this? Here we must be careful lest in our attempts to describe the matter we once again get seduced into inflating the magnificent hot-air balloon. Being freed from sin by the unconditional promise means that the totality of it begins to overwhelm and destroy our fundamental scepticism and incredulity, our unbelief. Lord, "I do believe; help me overcome my unbelief!" becomes our prayer (Mk 9:24). We can see light at the end of the tunnel. We begin to trust God rather than ourselves. When Martin Luther talked about these things, he began to talk more about our actual affections than lists of pious things to do.

Under the pressure of the total gift, we might actually begin to love God as God, *our* God, and to hate sin. Think of it: We might actually begin to *dislike* sin and to hope for its eventual removal. Ordinarily we feel guilty about our sins and fear their consequences, but we are far from *hating* them. I expect we do them, in spite of all fears and anxieties, because we like them. Sanctification under the invasion of the new, however, holds out the possibility of actually coming to hate sin, and to love God and his creation, or at least to make that little beginning. It is not that sin is taken away from us, but rather that we are to be taken away from sin—heart, soul and mind, as Luther put it.[6] In that manner, the law of God is to be fulfilled in us precisely by the uncompromising totality and unconditionality of the grace given.

[handwritten: Instead of us changing to be like Christ allow God to pull us away from sin]

Sanctification always comes from the whole, the totality. Whether it takes place in little steps, in isolated actions against particular sins, in those tender beginnings, it is always because of the invasion of the new. Always the totality is intensively there—the total crisis, the entire transition, the dying and becoming new.

What is the result of this? It should lead, I expect, to something of a reversal in our view of the Christian life. Instead of viewing ourselves on some kind of journey upward toward heaven, virtue and morality, our sanctification would be viewed more in terms of our journey back down to earth, the business of becoming human, the kind of creature God made. Our problem is that we have succumbed to the serpent's temptation, "You shall not die, you shall be as gods." Creation is not good enough for us; we are always on our way somewhere else. So we even look on sanctification in that light—our "progress" toward being "gods" of some sort. If what we have been saying is true, however, our salvation, our sanctification, consists in turning about and going the other way, getting back down to earth. The trouble we have is that it is a long way back for us. To get there we must learn to trust God, to be grasped by the totality of his grace, to become a creature, to become human.

[handwritten margin note: Human is? what ARE WE | Normal Humans? "Created in the image of God"]

What might that look like? When I think about such sanctification, I think about several things: spontaneity, taking care, vocation and attaining a certain elusive kind of truthfulness and lucidity about oneself. Perhaps I can end by saying a few words about these things.

Spontaneity

What is a truly good work, one that might qualify as the fruit of sanctification? One, I think, that is free, uncalculating, genuine, spontaneous. It would be like a mother who runs to pick up her child when it is hurt. There is no calculation, no wondering about progress, morality or virtue. There is just the doing of it, and then it is completely forgotten. The right hand doesn't know what the left is doing. Good works in God's eyes are quite likely to be all those things we have forgotten! True sanctification is God's secret.

Taking Care

If we are turned around to get back down to earth by grace, then it

[handwritten annotation: Quite opposite of today. Today the ME is taken out of / very brothers keeping and NS or them / is put in.]

would seem that true sanctification would show itself in taking care of our neighbor and God's creation, not exploiting and destroying either for our own ends, religious or otherwise. It would mean concern for the neighbor and society, caring for the other for the time being. Here one should talk about the place of morality and virtue and such things. Although we do not accept them as the means by which we are sanctified, they *are* the means by which and through which we care for the world and for the other. This is what the Reformers meant when they insisted that good works were to be done, but one was not to depend on them for salvation.

Vocation

How does the one who has died and is being made new, the one who has been taken off his or her own hands, enter into the battle in this world? The answer comes in the concept of carrying out one's vocation as a Christian in the tasks and occupations of daily life. We always get nervous about what we are to do, it seems. The magnificent hot-air balloon syndrome seduces us into thinking our sanctification consists in following lists of pious dos and don'ts. That always seems more holy. But it is in the nitty-gritty of daily life and its tasks that our sanctification is hammered out.

Precisely because of the totality of the gift, the new being knows that there is nothing to do to gain heaven. Thus the Christian is called to the tasks of daily life in this world, for the time being. Students, for instance, are sometimes very pious and idealistic about "doing something," and so get caught up in this or that movement "for good." It never seems to dawn on them that perhaps for the time being, at least, their calling is simply to be a good student! It is not particularly in acts of piety that we are sanctified, but in our call to live and act as Christians.

[handwritten margin note: Relationship of time to sanctification]

Truthfulness and Lucidity

In many ways, this essay has been an appeal for more truthfulness in our talk about the Christian life and sanctification. I think that should be the mark of sanctification as well. As Paul put it, we are not to think of ourselves more highly than we ought (Rom 12:3).

The talk of progress and growth we usually indulge in leads us all too often to do just that. But if we are saved and sanctified only by the unconditional grace of God, we ought to be able to become more truthful and lucid about the way things really are with us. Am I making progress? If I am really honest, it seems to me that the question is odd, even a little ridiculous. As I get older and death draws nearer, it doesn't seem to get any easier. I get a little more impatient, a little more anxious about having perhaps missed what this life has to offer, a little slower, harder to move, a little more sedentary and set in my ways. It seems more and more unjust to me that now that I have spent a good part of my life "getting to the top," and I seem just about to have made it, I am already slowing down, already on the way out. A skiing injury from when I was sixteen years old acts up if I overexert myself. I am too heavy, the doctors tell me, but it is so hard to lose weight! Am I making progress? Well, maybe it *seems* as though I sin less, but that may only be because I'm getting tired! It's just too hard to keep indulging the lusts of youth. Is that sanctification? I wouldn't think so! One should not, I expect, mistake encroaching senility for sanctification!

But can it be, perhaps, that it is precisely the unconditional gift of grace that helps me to see and admit all that? I hope so. The grace of God should lead us to see the truth about ourselves, and to gain a certain lucidity, a certain sense of humor, a certain down-to-earthness. When we come to realize that if we are going to be saved, it shall have to be absolutely by grace alone, then we shall be sanctified. God will have his way with us at last.

Notes

[1]Ernest Becker, *The Denial of Death* (New York: Free Press, 1973), p. 58.
[2]Alan Richardson, ed., *A Theological Wordbook of the Bible* (New York: Macmillan, 1960), p. 218.
[3]Eric Gritsch and Robert Jenson, *Lutheranism: The Theological Movement and Its Confessional Writings* (Philadelphia, Pa.: Fortress, 1976), pp. 8, 42.
[4]Martin Luther, *Lectures on Romans,* trans. and ed. Wilhelm Pauck, The Library of Christian Classics, vol. 15 (Philadelphia, Pa.: Westminster, 1961), p. 128.
[5]Ibid., p. 370.
[6]Ibid., p. 194.

A Reformed Response
Sinclair B. Ferguson

CHRISTIANS FROM NON-LUTHERAN TRADITIONS HAVE AL-
ways admired the sheer vitality of Luther's faith and the
expression of it in his theology. I appreciate the echo of this
in Dr. Forde's exposition.

Dr. Forde, following Luther, underscores the central role of justification. He is rightly concerned to stress that justification is *sola gratia*
(by grace alone). For this reason he defines sanctification as "getting
used to justification" and as unconditional in nature. He sees how
subtly Christians can smuggle works-righteousness into their salvation.

This concern to emphasize grace is shared by Reformed theology.
The desire to contribute *something* to our salvation is endemic to hu-
manity. Until we are finally delivered from the presence of sin, with all
its subtle deceptions to draw us back to works-righteousness, we will
constantly battle against it. Spiritual narcissism, as Dr. Forde points out
("How well is my sanctification going?"), can be a subtle form of this.
Luther dealt wisely with it when he said that "to progress [in the
Christian life] is to begin again" in the Christian life.

Within this context, there are several points at which the Reformed
edition of sanctification differs, more or less, from Dr. Forde's edition
of the Lutheran teaching.

1. I have the impression from the essay that so central is the idea of justification to Lutheran thought that it not only dominates sanctification, but at times even seems to threaten to displace the person of Christ from center stage. Justification is *in Christ,* and is to be sought in him, not in itself. In Reformed theology (and, I believe, in Scripture) this is a motif which is fundamental to justification.

Reformed theology sees the central role of justification as does Lutheran theology. It is "the main hinge on which religion turns" says Calvin; "the pivotal point around which everything moves" (Geerhardus Vos). But this justification is ours only through our union with Christ. This union is also the mainspring of our sanctification: Christ is both our righteousness (justification) and our sanctification (1 Cor 1:30 RSV).

When the doctrine of union with Christ is made the architectonic principle of the application of redemption (as it was in Calvin's thought [see *Institutes* 2.16.19], by contrast, I believe, with Luther), the tension which Lutheranism seems to feel *between* justification and the Christian's good works, or sanctification, begins to vanish. The one does not exist without the other, since both are effects of union with Christ. Yet neither is reduced to the other. Justification is not disgraced as though it were based on sanctification; sanctification is not demoted, as though it were a threat to the grace of justification.

The "I" who believes into union with Christ *(pisteuein eis)* is justified by grace; but being united to Christ, that same "I" has died to sin and has been raised to newness of life (Rom 6:3-23). We are justified by faith alone, but that faith is never alone in the one justified. This, it seems to me, is the thrust of James 2:14-26 (especially v. 24) which Luther found so difficult to grasp.

The fact that the good works of the believer are the "work of faith" (1 Thess 1:3; 2 Thess 1:11) itself safeguards them from compromising God's grace in salvation.

2. Dr. Forde stresses the unconditional nature of justification in order to safeguard its graciousness. He stresses that the form of the gospel is not "I will, *if*. . ." but "I will, *therefore*. . . ."

Reformed theology is as anxious as Lutheran thought to safeguard grace. It has wrestled very seriously with the whole question of conditions. The term *conditions* has a certain infelicity about it. But there is a difference between what we might call "conditionality" (which compromises grace by saying, "God will be gracious only if you do X or Y") and the fact that there are conditions for salvation which arise directly *out of* the gospel message and do not compromise its graciousness.

These conditions do not render God gracious to us, but are the noncontributory means by which we receive his grace. Our Lord himself says, "Unless you repent, you too will all perish" (Lk 13:3). Only *if* we suffer with Christ will we reign with him (Rom 8:17). "If we confess our sins, he is faithful and just and will forgive us our sins" (1 Jn 1:9). There is a *sine qua non* to forgiveness and to justification. They cannot be received apart from faith. This is a biblical condition that does not compromise grace, but arises from it. The important thing is not to deny conditions, but to underscore that "It is not faith that saves, but Christ that saves through faith" (B. B. Warfield).

3. Developing this point a little further, Lutheranism has had a deep reluctance to highlight the so-called "third use of the law" (as a rule for life). I appreciate Dr. Forde's concern to avoid a legalism that defines sanctification in formal terms.

In contrast, however, Reformed teaching speaks of "the grace of law." It recognizes the reappearance of the Decalogue in the New Testament's very concrete imperatives arising out of the gracious indicatives of the gospel (see, for example, Eph 6:1-3). This, Reformed theology argues, was the original context of the Decalogue itself (Ex 20:1). Obedience is nothing if it is not concrete and specific. Sanctification, ultimately Christlikeness, has a definite form and structure in the New Testament, as well as a foundation and motivation in grace. This in no wise detracts from the concern both Dr. Forde and Reformed theology share in stressing that sanctification is ultimately a true humanity, because it is ultimately likeness to our Lord Jesus Christ.

Restrictions of space meant that Dr. Forde did not expound the role of sacraments, fellowship and prayer in the Lutheran view of sanctification. I would have found comment on these particularly illuminating in view of, first, the way Luther's own life illustrates the principle that sanctification *is* prayer, and second, the historic differences between the Reformed and the Lutheran views of the church and the sacraments.

A Wesleyan Response
Laurence W. Wood

DR. *FORDE FOCUSES ON THE PRIORITY OF GRACE AND OUR* unconditional acceptance by God in Christ. He particularly perceives the need to stress human inability to achieve salvation. These are givens for any evangelical statement of faith. Yet too many believers have a theology of grace only in their heads, but a theology of works in their inner selves. The need to be self-reliant and to earn one's right to be called a child of God is a tacit feeling among believers and is itself a further indication of our sinful pride.

What all too often happens, even among Protestants, is that our doctrine of justification by faith through grace alone is nullified by our constant striving to earn our acceptance with God. Faith is a gift of God; we have only to accept our acceptance by God in Christ. We accept this acceptance because God empowers us to do so; it is not by human merit at all! If we reject it, we do so because God has empowered us to make a choice. In a sense, then, even our refusal of his gracious offer is made possible by his graciousness!

Wesley came to agree with Luther on the priority of grace. It was Luther's preface to his commentary on the book of Romans that was so decisive for Wesley. However, Wesley also came to see that while one is justified by faith, even so one could come to love God with all one's heart as a gift of grace as well. One is justified by faith; one is sanctified by faith. This work of sanctification is not something "added to justification"—a point Dr. Forde rightly makes. It is rather concomitant with justification and continues throughout the believer's life as he or she comes more and more to conform to the image of Christ.

So psychologically speaking, justification and sanctification occur simultaneously, but logically there is a clear distinction in their meaning, a distinction which Dr. Forde is reluctant to concede. Sanctification, by definition, means to be made holy. Justification means forgiveness of our sins. Sanctification is freedom from the being of sin; justification is freedom from the acts of sin. A twofold definition of sin assumed through the Scriptures (that is, we are sinners by nature and by choice) is the theological basis for this logical distinction between justification and sanctification. Now Dr. Forde perhaps implies this by acknowledging that sanctification is "getting used to justification."

However, Dr. Forde is worried about our tendency to seek salvation by our good works. This is certainly a valid concern, but perhaps in stressing the totality of grace and a kind of fideism that divorces faith from good works, Dr. Forde is engaging in an overreaction. Wesley contended with a kind of fideism in his day that led to antinomianism. The problem is not that one might fall into an antinomianism or a pharisaical works-righteousness, but whether or not one's life is actually renewed in the love of Christ. If so, obedience is an obvious mark of such an infusion of divine love.

One can hardly deny that the New Testament stresses obedience to God's commandments as a mark of discipleship. Dr. Forde's hesitancy to connect good works with sanctification reminds one of Luther's difficulty with the epistle of James, which Luther called an "epistle of straw." Certainly there is a dialectical tension between salvation by faith through grace alone and our Lord's commandment to do good works. Of course fulfilling the commandments of our Lord does not earn salvation for us, but if we are not obedient to his will this would certainly imply that we are no longer accepting his acceptance of us. God justifies and sanctifies freely and unconditionally. Our obedience to his will is a confirmation that we are indeed his children. If sanctification is being renewed in the image of Christ, then our behavior should reflect spiritual growth. We are "created in Christ Jesus to do good works" (Eph 2:10).

Incidentally, I suspect Protestants in general misinterpret the Council of Trent in its statement that we are justified by faith and good works. For Roman Catholic theology, justification has to do both with our initial acceptance of God in Christ and the entire life of the Christian until death. Consequently, in the end we will be justified if through faith and obedience we have so conducted our life. Perhaps, after all, Wesley was not that far away from his Anglo-Catholic roots when he stressed that justification by faith and a life lived in obedience to God were both necessary for salvation. In this respect, we are renewed in the image of Christ (sanctified) so that we are enabled to do good works.

Wesley believed that sanctifying grace occurred in the moment of justifying faith, but it continued throughout the believer's life. To be sure, somewhere along this continuum from justifying faith to the moment of the believer's death, the justified believer enters a union with Christ in an experience of perfect love (entire sanctification). This moment of pure love sparks a movement of growth in sanctifying grace in which the believer progressively becomes more and more like his Lord until death. There is no state of grace in this life in which one could claim that one had achieved total perfection. A Christian perfection of love is a dialectical process of always growing and increasing in love, knowledge and obedience to God.

This brings up another point, a problem of definition of terms. Dr. Forde refers to Luther's concept of the believer as one who is "simultaneously just and sinner." If sin means any deviation from the perfect will of God, then obviously all believers commit sin daily. However, if one were to substitute this definition for sin in almost all references in the New Testament (with the exception of a few places), then these texts would not make sense to us at all. For example, John says: "He who does what is sinful is of the devil" (Jn 3:8). If we translated this verse, "Whoever deviates from the perfect will of God is of the devil," then we must all despair of salvation, for all believers fall short of the perfect requirements of the law, daily and habitually. And John is making it quite clear here that believers do not commit "sin." Consequently, John could hardly have this kind of definition in mind.

This is why Wesley made a distinction between voluntary sins and involuntary sins. For Wesley, justified believers do not voluntarily sin against God. The assumption is that John is defining sin as a voluntary transgression against the known will of God. But if we do voluntarily transgress the will of God, we can still maintain fellowship with Christ if we seek forgiveness (1 Jn 2:1). Yet all believers must pray the Lord's prayer daily, "Forgive us our debts [sins]," because we all involuntarily transgress the perfect law of God. No saint, no matter how saintly, can claim to be sinless in this absolute sense.

Wesley rejected this idea of sinless perfection. And in this respect, Wesleyans make a distinction between the ethical concept of sin, which involves intention, and a legal concept of sin, which includes any infraction of the perfect will of God. Hence believers may love God with all their hearts, but they still must seek forgiveness and cleansing from their daily offenses. In this sense one is both a saint and a sinner.

Luther's assumption was that one cannot be freed from a sinful heart of pride. Hence one cannot truly love God with one's whole heart because the believer's love is still distorted by self-love. The Wesleyan tradition, along with the Anglo-Catholic tradition, perceives the New Testament to maintain a different stance; namely, that one *can* be justified and truly sanctified. Contemporary New Testament exegetes such as Krister Stendahl and Rudolf Bultmann maintain that Paul's overriding interest was not in justification by faith, but rather with sanctification by the Spirit. Not forgiveness of sins only, but freedom from sin itself was Paul's dominant motif.

Should a believer seek sanctification, or is this "God's hidden secret"? Dr. Forde is particularly concerned that if one "seeks" sanctification or if one testifies to being sanctified it would imply that salvation is a human attainment. Should one testify to being justified by faith through grace alone? Presumably such a testimonial is not dangerous or potentially disastrous because the emphasis is on "faith through grace." Dr. Forde apparently is reluctant to speak of sanctification because of the works-righteousness implied by such talk, but is it works-righteousness to testify to the belief that God has sanctified us by faith through grace alone? Paul says God had called him to preach the gospel of sanctification by faith (Acts 26:17-18). To the Thessalonians, Paul said he was righteous, blameless and holy (1 Thess 2:10).

To the Corinthians he claimed his conscience was clear, even though it is God alone who justifies us (1 Cor 4:4). To the Romans, writing in the rhetorical, historical present tense Paul acknowledges the inability of one to live righteously under the law without grace (Rom 7:7-24), but then Paul goes on to say we are liberated from sin and death (v. 25), and now we live in the age of the Spirit in which there is no condemnation and no more living according to the flesh (Rom 8:1-11). This holy living is a death to the old being and a renewing in the image of Christ (Romans 6—8).

This liberation is released within the believer through faith. Testimonials of God's grace always seem appropriate—if glory is given to God (Ps 107:2). Any actual righteousness in the believer is solely a gift of God. He declares us holy in Christ and actually makes the believer holy through the relationship the believer has with Christ. What makes the believer righteous is the relational dimension of sharing the love of Christ. Christ's love transforms the believer who in gratitude gives praise to God (Eph 5:15-20).

So we return to the question—should we seek sanctification? Hebrews 12:14 says: "Pursue peace with all men, and the sanctification without which no one will see the Lord" (NASB). Paul prayed for the Thessalonians that they might be sanctified entirely (1 Thess 5:23). Paul says it is holiness which establishes one in the faith (1 Thess 3:13). And his prayer for the Thessalonians was that they might be grounded in the love of God. To seek sanctification is a theological way of saying what one otherwise expresses devotionally in wanting to be more like Jesus as a loving and caring person. To seek sanctification is to pursue a deeper loving relationship with Christ. It is not something "added" onto justification, but an actualizing of what is already ours in Christ through his unconditional acceptance of us.

To be sure, God's acceptance of us and his forgiveness of our sins are not conditioned on anything we have done or could do to earn it. Yet there are conditions which grace places on us. If we accept God's offer, we shall be saved. If we reject God's offer, we will be lost. To receive God's offer of grace necessarily implies conditions—namely, that we do the will of God (1 Jn 2:17). That we choose to do the will of God and love him is a gift of God. We could not choose "for" or "against" grace—except as God empowers us to make a choice. We must bear the full consequences of the choices we make since God has given us that responsibility. That there are conditions imposed on us by grace is not a works-righteousness, but is part of the meaning of our personhood as responsible moral agents.

Dr. Forde makes it clear that we are obligated as Christians to grow in grace and that sin is to be conquered and expelled. He rightly insists that sanctification is the work of God. Perhaps my difficulty with his view has to do more with his focus on sanctification as secondary to justification by faith rather than seeing both emphases as essential aspects of the meaning of grace. "The grand depositum," which Wesley says God has given to Methodism, is the doctrine of holiness—a faith working by love. Luther restored for us the doctrine of justification by faith; Wesley's contribution to Protestant thought was his rediscovery of the meaning of sanctification by faith through grace alone.

Because of our different theological traditions, it is obvious that the significance of the related doctrines will be differently assessed. Believers in the Methodist tradition do not put justification and sanctification in competition with each other. Nor does Dr. Forde intend to. Yet it is clear that a distinctive of the Lutheran tradition is its helpful emphasis on justification, while a distinctive of the Wesleyan tradition is sanctification. Hopefully these distinctives can help us maintain a proper balance between the interrelated doctrines of justification and sanctification without downplaying the significance of either.

Finally, Dr. Forde's observations about the danger of a moralistic view of spirituality are to be taken seriously. Too often sanctification has degenerated into a legalistic list of dos and don'ts. The guilt-induced spiritual and psychological damage resulting from this kind of legalism is the exact opposite of grace. A genuine experience of grace releases us to be totally honest in our relationship to Christ. We can own our true feelings without pretentions, acknowledge our sins and grow in love because Christ totally accepts us. Sanctification is God's gift to us to enable us to enjoy communion with him. In this respect, Dr. Forde's emphasis on grace as opposed to legalism and moralism is helpful, but I believe Dr. Forde could have spoken more positively about what sanctification means to believers in their walk with Christ, and the positive and real changes this relationship brings to their inner being as they are renewed in the image of God.

A Pentecostal Response
Russell P. Spittler

S IMUL JUSTUS ET PECCATOR—*LOOSELY TRANSLATED "SAINT AND* sinner at the same time." Can Luther's formula be true?

I know what it is like to breathe this Lutheran air. My first graduate theological studies were undertaken at Concordia Seminary (pre-"Seminex") in St. Louis. To be saint and sinner at the same time wipes out effort: there's no need to pursue holiness. Striving ends. The message is: You've nothing to worry about. You'll never be "sanctified" anyway. Cool down and enjoy the ride.

A lot of Pentecostals need to hear that message. Particularly high-tech Wesleyan Pentecostals working on their third crisis experience. There's of course no necessary reason to get into a religious sweat working out the Pentecostal life. But it happens. The tradition is one that values experience; one that takes biblical mandates with utter seriousness; one that views sanctification as a definite state attainable through a specific crisis religious experience.

But can it really be true—saint and sinner simultaneously? I wish it were so. There's an authentic reflection of biblical truth here. But an imperfect one, I think.

What am I to make out of statements that sanctification is such good news that I need do nothing at all (no effort needed on my part) but "listen"? Nothing but listen? We'd have instant global revival if a tenth of the church for an hour running would really listen. And then call that "nothing at all" to do on my part? Such logic is too wonderful for me. And for many other Pentecostals, I judge.

I'll confess we have our bias equal in strength to the Lutheran. I'll confess as well that I've bought Luther's dictum enough to come down off the overly intense concern for personal holiness that I brought on myself through an overreading of my tradition's demands long ago. A bit of Luther's *simul* will do a lot for overbalanced believers submerged in their own heroic efforts at piety or bathed in what Roman Catholic moral theologians call "scrupulosity."

Is this correct: "I don't need to work at 'becoming.' I'm already declared to be holy. No sweat needed"? Similar logic marks a breed of Pentecostal (not my variety) that teaches that you'll have it if you'll only confess it. No sweat needed. It's already yours. "Positive confession" it's called. A derogatory parody puts it, "name it and claim it." Isn't the logic the same? Instant prosperity or effortless sanctification. Both look wrong to me.

I hear moral demands in Scripture. I take the imperatives with dead seriousness. I am a common man listening for the Word of God. I'm sure Dr. Forde means to make no case for antinomianism. But the Lutheran notion of sanctification as no more than "getting used to justification" looks to this Pentecostal like a clear steer down that road.

Still, I'm grateful for Luther's phrase and for his descendants. Their earthiness has called me away from my superspirituality.

But *simul justus et peccator*? I hope it's true! I simply fear it's not.

A Contemplative Response
E. Glenn Hinson

DR. *FORDE'S PAPER REFLECTS THE DISCOMFORT LUTHERANS* feel with the idea of sanctification. The concept which dominates his discussion is justification, defined in traditional Lutheran style as God's declaration of the sinner's acquittal on the basis of the saving work of Christ. "Sanctification is thus just the art of getting used to justification. It is not something added to justification."

To let any single concept dominate theology in this way is, to my mind, a questionable procedure. Behind it I detect an imperialism of Pauline theology (to which I will return in a moment). But even in the writings of the apostle the concepts "justification" and "sanctification" have different nuances. Although sanctification is linked to justification, it is not "just the art of getting used to justification," unless you define justification in a more comprehensive way than Dr. Forde does. Insofar as I can see, he still adheres to the juridical understanding of Luther and ignores the traditional Catholic view that justification also involves the transformation of the sinner. "God alone does the justifying simply by declaring the ungodly to be so, for Jesus' sake," Dr. Forde writes. Actually I don't know why it is any more dangerous to talk about sanctification apart from justification than it is to talk about justification in this constrictive sense. Yet most people I know who emphasize sanctification do not ignore justification; they simply have all they can handle when they deal with Christian growth.

Not being a Lutheran, I don't want to hack too hard on the doctrine of justification by faith alone, but I can't help sounding a warning about it in precisely the form Dr. Forde presents it. It would be more biblical to talk about justification by grace through faith. That, however, is not where the danger lies. The danger lies in "cheap grace." On this it suffices to cite a couple of perceptive Lutherans.

"As for the rest," inscribed Kierkegaard in his *Journal* in 1849, "the closer I examine Luther the more convinced do I become that he was muddle-headed. It is a comfortable kind of reforming which consists in throwing off burdens and making life easier—that is an easy way of getting one's friends to help. True reforming always means to make life more difficult, to lay on burdens; and the true reformer is therefore always put to death as though he were the enemy of mankind."

Dietrich Bonhoeffer was not so harsh on Luther, but rather on Lutherans. God raised up Luther "to restore the gospel of pure, costly grace," he observed in *The Cost of Discipleship* (Macmillan). Unfortunately, he went on to say, all too many of his followers interpreted the offer of "pure grace" as "a general dispensation from obedience to the command of Jesus," justification of sin rather than justification of the sinner. "Costly grace was turned into cheap grace without discipleship." Both "cheap grace" and "costly grace" use the same formula—"justification by faith alone." "Yet the misuse of the formula leads to the complete destruction of its very essence." Then comes the indictment: "We Lutherans have gathered like eagles round the carcass of cheap grace, and there we have drunk of the poison which has killed the life of following Christ." And Lutherans aren't the only ones.

Not only *justification* but also *grace* appears to me to be inadequately defined in Dr. Forde's essay. He describes grace in juridical terms as "the unconditional justification" which "*slays* the old self and destroys its 'body of sin,' so as to fashion a new one." I don't hear much about grace as God, the Risen Christ, present with us and empowering us to grow and develop. Dr. Forde doesn't seem to like the idea of perfection in love at all. Admitting that we will always remain "simultaneously just and sinner," I wonder whether we must stand still in this. Is there no forward progress? To deny any would be to ignore an awful

lot even of the apostle Paul's teaching, not to mention Matthew's or
the other Evangelists'. What, after all, is the thrust of Paul's prayer in
Philippians 1:9-11 save this very progress? "And this is my prayer: that
your love may abound more and more in knowledge and depth of
insight, so that you may be able to discern what is best and may be pure
and blameless until the day of Christ, filled with the fruit of righteousness that comes through Jesus Christ—to the glory and praise of God."

I wouldn't quibble at all with Dr. Forde's insistence that all of this
is "growth in grace." But once again he appears to take a narrow view
of grace, seeing it as something given rather than as the living God
invading our lives and transforming us. I'm not sure I can understand
at all how, as he contends, the goal moves toward us. When Paul talked
about this, he envisioned himself running in a race. He didn't consider
himself to have been already perfected or to have already arrived, but
he pressed on to attain that for which Christ had been taken hold of
him (Phil 3:12-16). This perspective surely fits better what the Gospels
teach us about the demands of discipleship than does Dr. Forde's dis-
suasion. According to Paul, grace is free and unconditional, but par-
adoxically, it costs everything. It costs you your life. To follow Jesus
you must deny self and take up a cross. The wise must count the cost.

With that I return to my earlier allusion to a Pauline imperialism.
Too much Protestant theology still subordinates the Gospels to Paul's
letters, usually the little package of Romans, 1 and 2 Corinthians and
Galatians. Brilliant as Paul was and great as his contribution was, I
wonder if we don't fly in the face of centuries of Christian wisdom
when we do this, and thus fail to listen to the whole counsel of God.
The Gospels give a rather different slant to things than did the apostle
to the Gentiles. We might struggle more with questions like these if
we listened to them alongside Paul, but we might also come closer to
the perspective we should hold.

The Reformed View

Sinclair B. Ferguson

R EFORMED THEOLOGY OWES A SPECIAL DEBT TO THE PRINCI-
ples of biblical exposition recovered for the church at the
time of the Reformation. It is particularly associated with
the work of John Calvin, but was later developed by such seventeenth-
century Puritans as John Owen and Thomas Goodwin (in England),
and Thomas Hooker and John Cotton (in New England). Many later
Christians have owed a special debt to the Reformed theological tradition. They include preachers like George Whitefield, C. H. Spurgeon
and D. Martyn Lloyd-Jones; and theologians such as Jonathan Edwards, Charles Hodge, Abraham Kuyper and B. B. Warfield; as well
as such influential twentieth-century Christian leaders as J. Gresham
Machen and Francis Schaeffer. From one point of view, most evangelical theology in the English-speaking world can be see as an exposition
of, deviation from or reaction to Reformed theology.[1]

A cursory glance at the biographies or writings of these men under-
lines the fact that Reformed theology has always placed special emphasis on the subject of sanctification. Few axioms are more central to
Reformed teaching than that theology and practice, doctrine and lifestyle are partners joined together by God. They ought never to be
separated. Nor is this relationship merely a "marriage of convenience."

It is one which Reformed theology sees as being "made in heaven," or more exactly, made in Scripture. A necessary connection between biblical doctrine and holy living is fundamental to the biblical and apostolic way of thinking. That is why Scripture is so full of moral imperatives logically derived from doctrinal indicatives: since these things are true, this is how you should live (compare Mt 6:32-34; Rom 12:1-2; Eph 4:20-25). The title of one of Francis A. Schaeffer's best-known books grows directly out of this Reformed appreciation of the shape of basic biblical teaching: *How Should We Then Live?* The "then" is pregnant with significance. It means "in light of the biblical teaching we know to be true, . . ." Indeed, in Schaeffer's case, it meant specifically "in the light of Reformed theology."

In fact, this marriage between what we believe and how we live was early illustrated by the *magnum opus* of Reformed theology, John Calvin's *Institutes of the Christian Religion.*[2] It was (and is) a manual to the teaching of Scripture. When Calvin first published it (at the tender age of 27), it bore the significant subtitle: *Containing the whole sum of piety.*[3] In apparent contrast to medieval works which bore the title *Sum of Theology (Summa Theologiae),* Calvin sought to engage the reader in an experiential fashion. His purpose was not only intellectual; it was also spiritual. One cannot read the *Institutes* without being impressed by this. Thus, from the beginning, Reformed theology has always emphasized sanctification. It could be said of many Reformed Christians, as it was actually said of John Owen, one of the finest Reformed theologians: "His aim in life was to promote holiness."[4]

What, then, are the distinctive features of the Reformed doctrine of sanctification? By definition (Reformed means reformed according to Scripture), these should also be the leading features of the Bible's own teaching. For this reason there are, thankfully, many points of contact and agreement between Reformed teaching and other perspectives. These should not be minimized; but the function of this essay is to express the chief emphases of the Reformed perspective.

Two features are central to sanctification: Jesus Christ himself is our sanctification or holiness (1 Cor 1:30); and it is through union with Christ that sanctification is accomplished in us. As Calvin says, "First we must understand that as long as Christ remains outside of us, and we are separated from him, all that he has suffered and done for the salvation of the human race remains useless and of no value to us."[5] But the phrase "Christ, our sanctification" has been variously understood. It is important, therefore, to notice that undergirding Calvin's statement are several strands of New Testament teaching.

Union with Christ

In the New Testament, Jesus is presented as the "author," "captain" or "pioneer" of salvation (Acts 3:15; 5:31; Heb 2:10; 12:2). The word *archēgos* (author) is notoriously difficult to translate into English.[6] In the case of Jesus (especially in the context of Hebrews) it seems to convey the twin notions of primacy and origin. Jesus is the "author" of our sanctification, in the sense that he creates it for us, but he is also its "pioneer" because he does so out of his own incarnate life, death and resurrection. He is the "pioneer" of our salvation, because as the Hero of Faith (to be distinguished from the long list of those heroes who bear witness to him [Heb 12:1]), he has endured the cross, despising its shame and the opposition of sinners, and is now seated at God's right hand. He is the first and only fully sanctified person. He has climbed God's holy hill with clean hands and a pure heart (Ps 24:3-6). It is as the "Lead Climber" that he gives the sanctification he has won to others (Acts 5:31). As "pioneer," Jesus has himself gone ahead of us to open up the way to the Father. By doing so, he brings to the Father in similar obedience all those who are "roped" to him by grace and faith.

Christ *is* our sanctification. In him it has first come to its fulfillment and consummation. He not only died for us to remove the penalty of our sin by taking it himself; he has lived, died, risen again and been exalted in order to sanctify our human nature in himself for our sake. This is the significance of his words shortly before the cross, "Sanctify [the disciples] by the truth. . . . As you sent me into the world, I have sent them into the world. For them I sanctify myself, that they too may be truly sanctified" (Jn 17:17-19).

Behind this lies a strand of teaching in the New Testament to which evangelicals have sometimes given insufficient emphasis—the notion that the Son of God took genuine human nature, "in the likeness of sinful man" (Rom 8:3), so that "Both the one who makes men holy and those who are made holy are of the same family" (Heb 2:11). Having sanctified his human nature from the moment of conception by his Spirit in the womb of the virgin Mary (Lk 1:35), Jesus lived his life of perfect holiness in our frail flesh set in a world of sin, temptation, evil and Satan. In our human nature, he grew in wisdom, in stature and in his capacity to obey the will of his Father.

As Jesus grew as a man, his human capacities developed, and with them the pressure of temptation (Lk 2:52). In that context he developed in obedience, not from imperfect to perfect, but from infancy to maturity. When he cried out on the cross "It is finished" (Jn 19:30; see also 17:4) and with royal dignity committed his spirit into the hands of his Father, he was the first person to have lived a life of perfect obedience and sanctification. In his resurrection his sanctified human life was divinely transformed into what the New Testament calls "the power of an indestructible life" (Heb 7:16). Because this has taken place first in Christ our representative, it is possible for it to take place also in us through the Spirit. Christ himself is the only adequate resource we have for the development of sanctification in our own lives.

Sanctification is therefore neither self-induced nor created in us by divine *fiat*. Like justification, it has to be "earthed" in our world (that is, in Christ's work for us in history) if it is to be more than a legal fiction. To change the metaphor, we can only draw on resources which have already been deposited in our name in the bank. But the whole of Christ's life, death, resurrection and exaltation have, by God's gracious design, provided the living deposit of his sanctified life, from which all our needs can be supplied. Because of our fellowship (union) with him we come to share his resources. That is why he can "become for us" sanctification, just as he is also our wisdom, righteousness and redemption (1 Cor 1:30).

No one has expressed the riches of this biblical teaching more eloquently than Calvin himself:

We see that our whole salvation and all its parts are comprehended in Christ [Acts 4:12]. We should therefore take care not to derive the least portion of it from anywhere else. If we seek salvation, we are taught by the very name of Jesus that it is "of him" [1 Cor 1:30]. If we seek any other gifts of the Spirit, they will be found in his anointing. If we seek strength, it lies in his dominion; if purity, in his conception; if gentleness, it appears in his birth. For by his birth he was made like us in all respects [Heb 2:17] that he might learn to feel our pain [compare to Heb 5:2]. If we seek redemption, it lies in his passion; if acquittal, in his condemnation; if remission of the curse, in his cross [Gal 3:13]; if satisfaction, in his sacrifice; if purification, in his blood; if reconciliation, in his descent into hell; if mortification of the flesh, in his tomb; if newness of life, in his resurrection; if immortality, in the same; if inheritance of the Heavenly Kingdom, in his entrance into heaven; if protection, if security, if abundant supply of all blessings, in his Kingdom; if untroubled expectation of judgment, in the power given to him to judge. In short, since rich store of every kind of good abounds in him, let us drink our fill from this fountain, and from no other.[7]

If Calvin is right, then the dynamic for sanctification, indeed for the whole life of the Christian, is to be found in union with Christ.

The Effecting of the Union

In Christ's incarnate, crucified, risen and glorified humanity lies the sanctification I lack in myself. The question therefore becomes: How are his sanctification and my need for it brought together?

According to the New Testament, it is by the ministry of God's Spirit and by the exercise of the believer's faith. Union with Christ is the purpose and one of the foci of the ministry of the Spirit. Jesus emphasized that the Spirit "will bring glory to me by taking from what is mine and making it known to you" (Jn 16:14). This was to be realized when the Father would give the apostles the Spirit, the Counselor, to be with them forever (that is, on the Day of Pentecost: "On *that* day you will realize that I am in my Father, *and you are in me, and I am in you*" [Jn 14:20, emphasis mine]). The coming of the Spirit ("baptism with the Spirit") on the Day of Pentecost is the means by which the disciples are united to Christ.

But this union with Christ does not take place over our heads, as it were. It engages our whole being. Consequently, a second element in it is that of *faith*. In the New Testament's language, we believe *into* Christ *(pisteuein eis),* that is, into union with him. Faith involves trusting in and resting on the resources of Christ as though they were our own.

The first disciples' experience in this context was obviously in some elements unique. They alone belonged to the time before and after Christ. Like other believers of the Old Testament era, they were regenerated before the death, resurrection, ascension and Pentecost events (and in some sense, united to Christ [compare Jn 15:3-5; 13:10]). But, like believers in all ages thereafter, they also received the Spirit of the *ascended* Christ, an event which (in their case necessarily) was chronologically separated from their regeneration. Their entrance into all that union with Christ means to New Testament believers was therefore progressive. By contrast, for Christians after the initial period of overlap between the Old and New epochs of redemption, the experiences of faith, regeneration *and* baptism with the Spirit take place simultaneously—a threefold perspective on the one event in which no perspective is simply reducible to either of the other two.

Union and Sanctification

How does this union have significance for sanctification? Or are Calvin's eloquent words, cited above, simply a theologian's rhetoric? The fact that union with Christ has profound significance lies on the surface of the New Testament. In the crisis hours before his arrest, Jesus gave his disciples careful instruction on this theme (Jn 14:20; 15:1-4; 17:23). Similarly, in dealing with pressing pastoral problems, Paul frequently reminds his readers of their union with Christ as the solvent of their situation and the ground of his own exhortations to them (compare to Rom 6:1-14; Gal 2:20-21; Eph 2:1-6; Col 2:6—3:17). On the basis of such passages the Westminster Confession of Faith, for example, is able to say:

> They who are effectually called and regenerated, having a new heart and a new spirit created in them, are farther sanctified really and personally, *through the virtue of Christ's death and resurrection.*[8] (emphasis mine)

The most meticulously logical development of this appears in Romans 6:1-14.

> What shall we say, then? Shall we go on sinning so that grace may increase? By no means! We died to sin; how can we live in it any longer? Or don't you know that all of us who were baptized into Christ Jesus were baptized into his death? We were therefore buried with him through baptism into death in order that, just as Christ

was raised from the dead through the glory of the Father, we too may live a new life.

If we have been united with him like this in his death, we will certainly also be united with him in his resurrection. For we know that our old self was crucified with him so that the body of sin might be done away with, that we should no longer be slaves to sin—because anyone who has died has been freed from sin.

Now if we died with Christ, we believe that we will also live with him. For we know that since Christ was raised from the dead, he cannot die again; death no longer has mastery over him. The death he died, he died to sin once for all; but the life he lives, he lives to God.

In the same way, count yourselves dead to sin but alive to God in Christ Jesus. Therefore do not let sin reign in your mortal body so that you obey its evil desires. Do not offer the parts of your body to sin, as instruments of wickedness, but rather offer yourselves to God, as those who have been brought from death to life; and offer the parts of your body to him as instruments of righteousness. For sin shall not be your master, because you are not under law, but under grace.

The complexity of Paul's logic in this passage is obvious. He has just been expounding the central fact of redemptive history: what was forfeited in Adam has been regained in the Last Adam, Jesus Christ (Rom 5:12-21). The principle is that where sin increased, the grace of God has increased all the more (Rom 5:20). To this there is an obvious retort: "Shall we continue sinning, therefore? For if increased sin evokes increased grace, does it not follow that our indulgence in sin will promote grace and therefore enhance the glory of God?"

Such a response is a monstrous misunderstanding of the gospel. Paul's reaction is as violent as it is theological. For the forgiveness of sins is not received in a vacuum, but in union with Christ ("In him we have redemption through his blood, the forgiveness of sins" [Eph 1:7]). But if we have been united to Christ, we share in him as a crucified and risen savior. When he was crucified, he died to sin; when he was resurrected, he was raised to new life with the Father (Rom 6:8-10). If in becoming Christians we have been united to *this* Christ, it follows that (in some sense) we have died to sin with him and been

raised similarly into a new life. This being the case, how can those who
have received forgiveness in Christ, and are thus united to him, go on
living in sin? They do not. Indeed, Paul's point is that they *cannot*
because they have died to sin.

Paul's logic is impeccable:

1. We receive forgiveness of sins through Christ.
2. This reception involves being united to Christ.
3. The Christ to whom we are united, died to sin.
4. Since we are united to him, we also have died to sin.
5. If we have died to sin, we cannot continue living in it.
6. Therefore, we cannot continue in sin that grace may increase.

Justification is received by faith alone, but since that faith unites us to
Christ as sanctifier, justification and sanctification can no more be
separated than Christ himself can be divided.

Death to Sin

While Paul's logic is flawless, his interpreters have found his teaching
sufficiently obscure to give rise to a variety of interpretations of it. In
particular, his idea of the believer as one who is "dead to sin" has
frequently been abused to suggest various forms of perfectionism.
Here even Homer nods, when in his often masterly paraphrase of
Romans, J. B. Phillips translates Romans 6:7 as: "a dead man can safely
be said to be immune to the power of sin." But both Scripture and
experience make it abundantly clear that Christians can "safely" be said
not to be immune to the power of sin!

Again, it is sometimes suggested that the key to sanctification lies
in Paul's command to count oneself "dead to sin." Defeat in the Christian life is therefore attributed to a failure to enter into a new stage of
experience altogether in which sin is no longer a serious challenge to
the Christian. But this is the high road to theological and pastoral, as
well as psychological, shipwreck. The notion that we have died to sin
and are alive to God lies at the heart of the biblical doctrine of sanctification. Death to sin and life to God *is* sanctification. But what is the
nature of this death and life?

Reformed theology has not answered that question with a completely harmonious voice exegetically; but theologically and pastorally the
response has been relatively constant. Even an outline of its chief fea-

tures underscores the fact that Reformed theology has stressed the cosmic context in which Scripture expounds sanctification.

In the immediate context in Romans, Paul has been expounding the work of Christ and his grace by contrasting them with Adam and his Fall. Through Adam, sin and death have come into the world. But such is the divinely instituted relationship between Adam and his posterity, the human race, that persons by nature are "in Adam." He has acted as their head and representative. Consequently, through his one act of disobedience, all persons in Adam have come under the power of sin and death (compare to Rom 5:12; 1 Cor 15:22). This is the ultimate foundation for, and explanation of, the fact that humanity is unsanctified before God. "There is no one righteous, not even one. . . . No one will be declared righteous in his sight. . . . All have sinned and fall short of the glory of God" (Rom 3:10-23). This situation is encapsulated in Paul's statement that "sin reigned" (Rom 5:21).

Throughout Romans 5 and 6, Paul uses the definite article with the word sin *(hē hamartia)*, perhaps suggesting that sin is to be thought of as a personified power or as a realm in which humans live. It reigns as a king (5:21; 6:12) and makes people serve it as their master (6:14) so that they are sin's slaves (6:17, 20). It is a warring general who uses people's bodies as his weapons *(hopla* 6:13); it is an employer who pays wages at the end of the day—but "the wages of sin is death" (6:23).

Against this background it becomes clearer what death to sin *does not* mean. It does not describe an activity which the Christian must perform (die to sin!), for the verb is in the indicative mood, not the imperative. Paul is not telling us we are to do something; he is analyzing something that has taken place.

Nor does death to sin mean that we are no longer capable of committing any acts of sin. Not only would that contradict the teaching of Scripture elsewhere (for example, 1 Jn 1:8-10) and run counter to actual experience, it would make nonsense of Paul's urgent exhortations in this very passage to cease sinning. "Do not let sin reign" and "Do not offer the parts of your body to sin" (Rom 6:12-13) suggest that the Christian continues to battle with it.

Freed from Sin

What, then, does Paul mean? He explains in verse 7: "Anyone who has died has been freed from sin." Two different interpretations of his words have been adopted by Reformed theologians.

First, Paul's words in this verse *(ho gar apothanōn dedikaiōtai apo tēs hamartias)* may be narrowly interpreted to mean: "For the one who has died is *justified* from his sin." In this case Paul is saying that sharing in Christ's death for sin means being released from bearing the burden of guilt for sin ourselves.[9]

Alternatively, Paul's words may mean: "The one who has died (with Christ) is not merely justified, but has also been set free from the reign, or dominion of sin." There are solid reasons for accepting this second interpretation:

1. At this point in the context of Romans 6, Paul is speaking about the dominion or reign of sin; his concern is with the authority of sin over us, not its guilt. The point at issue is whether Christians continue to live under the reign of sin as they formerly did. Since Paul's general argument is that Christians are delivered from the reign of sin (although not its continuing presence), "set free" from sin is the more relevant concept.

2. Later in the passage (6:18), Paul specifically expounds the significance of union with Christ in terms of freedom from sin: "You have been set free from sin and have become slaves of righteousness." Here the context is clearly one of deliverance from bondage, not alleviation of guilt, and the term Paul uses *(eleutherothentes)* implies such freedom.

Against this view it is sometimes argued that proper exegesis demands the conclusion that the believer has died to sin in the same sense that Christ is said to have died ("The death he died, he died to sin once for all" [Rom 6:10]). Christ could not die to sin except in the sense of bearing its guilt, it is argued.

But Paul has already indicated that sin's reign is expressed in death. Insofar as Christ died for us, we must say that he submitted himself not only to death, but to the reign of sin through death. He too died to sin, in the sense of dying to its reign over him. It may further clarify Paul's thinking here if we remember that for him, the resurrection involved Christ's deliverance (his vindication, or justification) from the reign of sin in death (1 Tim 3:16). In union with him, we too are delivered from sin's reign as a tyrant-king as well as from sin's guilt. Only because we are free from both are we in any position to resist the remaining presence of sin.

In view of this, Paul says: "Sin shall not be your master" (Rom 6:14). This indicative-mood statement forms the basis for the radical impera-tives which Paul issues to those who have thus died to sin and are now alive to God.[10]

We may follow Paul further. Not only is this "death to sin" deliv-erance from its dominion—and something which has already been ac-complished, rather than an injunction to be obeyed—it is a fundamen-tal and universal principle of sanctification for every Christian. Indeed, it is so true of each and every Christian as to be virtually definitive of *being* a Christian. "All of us who were baptized into Christ Jesus" (all Christians) have thus died to sin. "We died to sin" *(hoitines apethanomen tē hamartia)* might be more fully rendered: "We *who are the kind of people who* died to sin," that is, "we—who have this as one of our leading characteristics—have died to sin."[11] Therefore we are to act "as those who have been brought from death to life" (6:13; "as dead men brought to life" is C. K. Barrett's fine rendering).

This is so because "we have been united with [Christ] in his death" (v. 5). Here again Paul's language is illuminating. His use of *sumphutos (sun,* along with; *phuo,* to bring forth, beget, and in the passive, to spring up or grow) suggests that we share one bundle of life with Christ in what he has done.[12] All that he has accomplished for us in our human nature is, through union with him, true for us and, in a sense, of us. He died to sin once; he lives to God (6:10). He came under the dominion of sin in death, but death could not master him. He rose and broke the power of both sin and death. Now he lives forever in resurrection life to God. The same is as true of us as if we had been with him on the cross, in the tomb and on the resurrection morning!

We miss the radical nature of Paul's teaching here to our great loss. So startling is it that we need to find a startling manner of expressing it. For what Paul is saying is that sanctification means this: in relation-ship both to sin and to God, the determining factor of my existence is *no longer my past. It is Christ's past.* The basic framework of my new existence in Christ is that I have become a "dead man brought to life" and must think of myself in those terms: dead to sin and alive to God in union with Jesus Christ our Lord.

Precisely at this juncture, however, personal experience tends to intrude. As Christians we continue to sin. And the danger is that we may think that the sinful lifestyle is still *normative* for us. We thus obscure the power of the gospel by focusing attention on the remaining sin in our lives. But for the New Testament, that view of the Christian life is to look at grace through the wrong end of the telescope. No one has expressed this with more accurate eloquence than John Murray:

> We are too ready to give heed to what we deem to be the hard, empirical facts of Christian profession, and we have erased the clear line of demarcation which Scripture defines. As a result we have lost our vision of the high calling of God in Christ Jesus. Our ethic has lost its dynamic and we have become conformed to this world. We know not the power of death to sin in the death of Christ, and we are not able to bear the rigour of the liberty of redemptive emancipation.[13]

A similar point was made three hundred years earlier by the great Puritan theologian John Owen. He saw two major pastoral burdens to be: "To convince those in whom sin evidently hath the dominion that such indeed is their state and condition"; and "To satisfy some that sin hath not the dominion over them, notwithstanding its restless acting itself in them and warring against their souls; *yet unless this can be done, it is impossible they should enjoy solid peace and omfort in this life*"[14] (emphasis mine).

A New Creation

Union with Christ in his death and resurrection is the element of union which Paul most extensively expounds. But the principle of Romans 6 is a wider one: if we are united to Christ, then we are united to him at all points of his activity on our behalf. We share in his death (we were baptized into his death), in his burial (we were buried with him in baptism), in his resurrection (we are resurrected with Christ), in his ascension (we have been raised with him), in his heavenly session (we sit with him in heavenly places, so that our life is hidden with Christ in God) and we will share in his promised return (when Christ, who is our life, appears, we also will appear with him in glory) (Rom 6:14; Col 2:11-12; 3:1-3).

This, then, is the foundation of sanctification in Reformed theology. It is rooted, not in humanity and their achievement of holiness or sanctification, but in what God has done in Christ, and for us in union with him. Rather than view Christians first and foremost in the microcosmic context of their own progress, the Reformed doctrine first of all sets them in the macrocosm of God's activity in redemptive history. It is seeing oneself in this context that enables the individual Christian to grow in true holiness.

This general approach is well illustrated by Paul's key statements: "We know that our old self [*anthrōpos,* man] was crucified with [Christ] so that the body of sin might be done away with, that we should no longer be slaves to sin" (Rom 6:6).

What is here said to be accomplished already is the central element in sanctification (we are no longer slaves to sin, we are servants of God). It is accomplished by doing away with "the body of sin"—an expression which may refer in the context of Romans 6 to the physical body, or more generally, to bodily existence as the sphere in which sin's dominion is expressed. In Christ, sin's status is changed from that of a citizen with full rights to that of an illegal alien (with no rights—but for all that, not easily removed!). The foundation of this is what Paul describes as the co-crucifixion with Christ of the old man.

The "old man" *(ho palaios anthrōpos)* has often been taken to refer to what I was before I became a Christian ("my former self"). That is undoubtedly implied in the expression. But Paul has a larger canvas in mind here. He has been expounding the fact that men and women are "in Adam" or "in Christ." To be "in Adam" is to belong to the world of the "old man," to be "in the flesh," a slave to sin and liable to death and judgment. From this perspective, Paul sees Jesus Christ as the Second Man, the Last Adam, the New Man. He is the first of a new race of humans who share in his righteousness and holiness. He is the first of the New Age, the Head of the New Humanity, through his resurrection (compare to 1 Cor 15:45-49). By grace and faith we belong to him. We too share in the new humanity. If we are in Christ, we share in the new creation (2 Cor 5:17), we are no longer "in the flesh," but "in the Spirit." The life and power of the resurrection age have already begun to make their presence felt in our life.

What is so significant here is the transformation this brings to the Christian's self-understanding. We do not see ourselves merely within the limited vision of our own biographies: volume one, the life of slavery in sin; volume two, the life of freedom from sin. We see ourselves set in a cosmic context: in Adam by nature, in Christ by grace; in the old humanity by sin, in the new humanity by regeneration. Once we lived under sin's reign; now we have died to its rule and are living to God. Our regeneration is an event of this magnitude! Paul gropes for a parallel to such an exercise of divine power and finds it in two places: the creation of the world (2 Cor 4:6; 5:17) and the resurrection and ascension of Christ (Eph 1:19-20).

Against this background Paul urges radical consecration and sanctification (Rom 6:11-14). In essence his position is that the magnitude of what God has accomplished is itself adequate motivation for the radical holiness which should characterize our lives.

In actual practice, it is the dawning of this perspective which is the foundation for all practical sanctification. Hence Paul's emphasis on "knowing" that this is the case (vv. 3, 6, 9), and his summons to believers to "count" themselves dead to sin and alive to God in Christ Jesus (v. 11). "Count" ("reckon," KJV) does not mean to bring this situation into being by a special act of faith. It means to recognize that such a situation exists and to act accordingly.

Sanctification is therefore the consistent practical outworking of what it means to belong to the new creation in Christ. That is why so much of the New Testament's response to pastoral and personal problems in the early church was: "Do you not know what is true of you in Christ?" (Rom 6:3, 16; 7:1; 1 Cor 3:16; 5:6; 6:2-3, 9, 14, 19; 9:13, 24). "Live by the Spirit's power in a manner that is consistent with that! If you have died with Christ to sin and been raised into new life, quit sinning and live in a new way. If, when Christ appears, you will appear with him and be like him, live now in a manner that conforms to your final destiny!"

Spiritual Warfare

When the groundwork of sanctification is seen in this light, its progress is inevitably marked by conflict or tension. By contrast with teaching which emphasizes that the chief characteristic of the Christian life is *quietness* (physical, mental or spiritual), Reformed theology has stressed pilgrimage *(Pilgrim's Progress)* and conflict ("The Holy War"). Such conflict is not viewed as either an unfortunate malfunction or the result of a lack of faith or spirituality. Rather, conflict is inherent in the very nature of the glory of what God has already done for us. The magnitude of grace, when it impacts fallen humanity in a fallen world, inevitably produces conflict.

The New Testament provides several perspectives on this conflict which together present a unified picture.

The conflict is the result of our now being *in Christ* and yet, at the same time, living *in the world* (compare 1 Cor 1:2, "in Corinth" and "in Christ Jesus"). Since by nature we were dead in sin and used to live according to the fashions of this world, gratifying our own lusts (Eph 2:1-3), our new lifestyle in Christ is bound to be on a collision course with the lifestyle of this world. Why else would Paul "insist . . . that [we] must no longer live as the Gentiles do" (Eph 4:17)? The goals, motives and energies of our lives now stand in complete contrast to the world around us. That radical difference makes tension, conflict, even stress inevitable (compare to 2 Tim 3:1-9).

A further biblical element in this conflict which Reformed theology has consistently sought to emphasize has been the opposition of Satan to Christian growth. What is true of the reign of sin is also true of the dominion of darkness. We have been freed from it, yet its presence is not finally destroyed. Rendered ultimately powerless (Heb 2:14, where the same verb *[katargeō]* appears as in Rom 6:6 in connection with the destruction of the body of sin), Satan continues to menace Christians. He seeks, says Calvin in connection with Job, "to drive the saint to madness by despair."[15] He is the hinderer, the enemy, the accuser, the tempter, the devourer. He seduces, deceives and tempts us with his many wiles.

Reformed literature therefore contains many serious manuals to serve the Christian soldier.[16] Here again we find the New Testament's emphasis on sanctification taking place in a cosmic context. We have "received every spiritual blessing in Christ . . . in the heavenly realms" (Eph 1:3, also v. 20). But now that we are united to him we are immediately involved in a conflict which is engaged precisely in the same heavenly realms (Eph 6:12). Our daily lives involve the skirmishes of the eschatological war of the end times. For this reason we need to wear all the armor of God, so that "when the evil day comes" we may remain standing.

But the conflict is not only external and objective; it is internal and subjective—with the flesh as well as with the world and the devil. All that is true *for me* in Christ has not yet been accomplished *in me* by the Spirit. I live in the Spirit, but I also continue to live in the flesh (though no longer dominated by it, nor a debtor to it). But as I have been delivered from bondage to the flesh, I continue to live my life with a body and mind marred by sin, and in a world and community which have been dominated by the flesh. Although I have been delivered from addiction to sin, its presence remains. I experience withdrawal symptoms and remain weakened by its devastating impact on my life. The desires of the flesh and the desires of the Spirit are contrary to one another. Whatever view I would like to take of my own degree of sanctification, I know that there are times when Paul's words ring true: "You do not do what you want" (Gal 5:17). In microcosm, I experience a reflection of the conflict between the kingdom of God and the kingdoms of this world. Because I am destined for the glory of Christ, so long as I am in the body, I groan, longing for the day when my life as a child of God will be brought to its final consummation (Rom 8:23).

In this context, especially in more recent years, Reformed exegesis has not been unanimous in its interpretation of Romans 7:14-25. In the post-Reformation centuries, it has been normal, if not normative, to understand Paul's words as a description of a regenerate person. Despite trends to the contrary, my opinion is that this remains the best approach to understanding the passage.[17] It does, however, need to be underlined (as it has not always been in Reformed or any other tradition or interpretation) that while what Paul says in Romans 7:14-25 may be true of him as a believer, *it is not the only way of describing his experience as a believer.* At the heart of Romans 7:14-25 is a profound paradox, both elements of which must be recognized. As G. C. Berkouwer has written: "Whoever thinks he has been treated [in Rom 7:14-25] to an intolerable contradiction is probably the victim of the effort to make this duality psychologically transparent. He is a dupe indeed: there is no transparency here, only grief over sin, meekness, confession of guilt, and a glory in salvation."[18] For Paul is viewing himself within a particular context—his continued imperfection when judged by the spiritual standards of the divine law.

But whether Romans 7:14-25 in particular is Paul speaking as a Christian or not, *it is a strange Christian who has not at some time realized that everything Paul describes is also experienced by all Christians.*

So long as we are in the body, in this world, will we find ourselves crying out from time to time: "What a wretched man I am! Who will rescue me from this body of death? Thanks be to God—through Jesus Christ our Lord!" (Rom 7:24-25). Our sanest conclusion about our present status as believers will be: "I myself in my mind am a slave to God's law, but in the sinful nature [*sarx* = flesh] a slave to the law of sin" (Rom 7:25). No other interpretation does justice to the remarkable combination of Paul's cry of victory and his recognition of the reality of sin's continuing influence via the flesh in Romans 7:25.[19] Nor is this pessimism. Indeed it is biblical realism. It is the inevitable concomitant of a glorious redemption already inaugurated but not yet consummated. The greater the glory, the greater the contrast with all that has not yet been glorified.

Partly in reaction to such a serious (and dark) emphasis, some have been tempted to stress the way in which the Spirit of God lifts the believer beyond this plane of experience. In response, Reformed theologians have sought to say, graciously but firmly, that while the dispensation of the Spirit is indeed glorious (2 Cor 3:7-11), it is seriously mistaken to conclude that the presence of the Spirit will keep us from sin. It illustrates the difficulty we have in accepting the tensions produced by the present incompleteness of God's work in us, in view of the completeness of his work for us in Christ. But the biblical response to the view that the Spirit raises God's people above those conflicts is that in fact *it is the presence of the Spirit that produces these conflicts.*

It is those who have the first fruits of the Spirit who groan inwardly as they wait eagerly (note the balance!) for their final redemption (Rom 8:23). Here "first fruits" does not mean that we have only a little of the spirit and we need more if we are to cease groaning and enter into victory. The Spirit himself is the first fruits of glory. No one can be possessed by him without being caught up in the contrast between flesh and Spirit.

Necessary Mortification
This conflict, inherent in sanctification prior to glorification (final

sanctification), in turn provides the proper context for a further feature of the Reformed doctrine of sanctification: the necessity of mortification.

The Latinate nature of the term "mortification" suggests the world of the medieval, the monastic and the masochistic. At times Christians have mistakenly resorted to weapons of the flesh rather than the sword of the Spirit to deal with sin. But again at this point, Reformed theology has sought to maintain a biblical balance, recognizing the continuing presence of sin in the believer and Scripture's frequent exhortations to deal with it severely. Wrong views of sanctification can frequently be traced to misunderstanding the nature of sin in the Christian.

In the New Testament, mortification is not a form of legalism (as Col 2:9-23 emphasizes), but a repercussion of divine blessing. It is those who belong to the kingdom of God as "beatitude people" (Mt 5:1-12) who are urged to deal rigorously with sin (Mt 5:21-48), to cut off or pluck out whatever is a source of temptation. It is those who are united to Christ in his death, resurrection, ascension, session and coming glory who are urged to "put to death, *therefore,* whatever belongs to your earthly nature," whether it be mental acts or physical deeds (Col 3:5-11).

Since Christians have put off the old man and put on the new man, they should live accordingly (Col 3:9-10). It is those who have received God's promises who should purify themselves "from everything that contaminates body and spirit, perfecting holiness out of reverence for God" (2 Cor 7:1). It is the person who has the hope that "when [Jesus] appears, we shall be like him, for we shall see him as he is" and who "purifies himself, just as [Jesus] is pure" (1 Jn 3:1-3). It is the one who already possesses the Holy Spirit as the gift of God's future kingdom, who by that Spirit is to "put to death the misdeeds of the body" (Rom 8:13). "Those who belong to Christ Jesus have crucified the sinful nature with its passions and desires" (Gal 5:24).

Grace demands mortification. Without it there is no holiness. John Owen writes graphically: "Let not that man think he makes any progress in true holiness who walks not over the bellies of his lusts."[20]

Mortification is the outworking of our union with Christ in his death to sin. But that must not be limited to our interior life. There is in the New Testament what Calvin called an internal and an external mortification. Bearing the cross involves crucifying the lusts of the flesh. The providential experiences of life serve a similar function. Just as we put sin to death in order to live (Rom 8:13), so God sends painful providences in order that new life may arise both in us and in others. This external mortification is described variously. It involves bearing the cross; it is the Father's pruning in order that we may bear more fruit (Jn 15:2); it is described supremely in Paul's remarkable words in 2 Corinthians 4:7-12:

> We have this treasure in jars of clay to show that this all-surpassing power is from God and not from us. We are hard pressed on every side, but not crushed; perplexed, but not in despair; persecuted, but not abandoned; struck down, but not destroyed. We always carry around in our body the death of Jesus, so that the life of Jesus may also be revealed in our body. For we who are alive are always being given over to death for Jesus' sake, so that his life may be revealed in our mortal body. So then, death is at work in us, but life is at work in you.

Union with Christ is not an inner mysticism. It affects the whole person. The silhouette of Christ's life marks all of the Christian's experience. Our personal *Sitz im Leben* becomes the instrument God uses to work out the realities of our union with Christ. Thus, Louis Berkhof has written:

> By this union believers are changed into the image of Christ *according to his human nature*. What Christ effects in his people is in a sense a replica or reproduction of what took place with Him. Not only objectively, but also in a subjective sense they suffer, bear the cross, are crucified, die and are raised to newness of life with Christ. They share in a measure the experiences of their Lord.[21]

Imitation and Self-Evaluation

The ground plan of sanctification, union with Christ, is prophetic of the divine goal in sanctification: renewal in the image of Christ. "For those God foreknew he also predestined to be conformed to the likeness of his Son, that be might be the firstborn among many brothers" (Rom 8:29). The whole schema of redemptive history has this in view.

Humans by creation were made as the image of God, and called to

[handwritten margin notes: "Our lives are a Reflection of the Redemptive History of God Past → Present → Future, Adam → Christ crucified → Christ Resurrected"]

express that image as offspring and reflectors of the divine glory. We sinned and fell short of the glory of God. Thus Adam and Eve became prodigals. In Christ, glory and sonship are restored (he was declared to be the Son with power when he was raised from the dead by the glory of the Father [Rom 1:4; 6:4]). Through Spirit-union with Christ in the epochal events which brought him to the new humanity of the resurrection, we are already being conformed to his image—from one degree of glory to the next (2 Cor 3:18).

The corresponding responsibility for the believer is the imitation of Christ. Like mortification, this is a notion which, because of its abuse, has often fallen into disuse among evangelical Christians. But it is thoroughly biblical. Union with Christ for the Thessalonians meant that they "became imitators of the Lord" (1 Thess 1:6). We are to have the "mind of Christ" (1 Cor 2:16), who left his disciples an example, "that you should do as I have done for you" (Jn 13:15). When Peter urges slaves to live as Christians, he tells them: "Christ suffered for you, leaving you an example, that you should follow in his steps" (1 Pet 2:21). Peter is applying to slaves a general principle which governs all Christian living. His language is graphic: *example* (*hupogrammos*, or "write under") is the word for a written copy. It belongs to the world of elementary education, where the teacher writes letters on one line and tells the child to copy them on the next line. Peter is urging Christians to write the biography of their own lives with one eye on the lifestyle which Jesus had written. Imitation of the incarnate Savior is the essence of continuing sanctification.

Because sanctification involves the imitation of Christ, its goal is true humanity, regained through Christ. That this is the heart of the Reformed doctrine of sanctification cannot be overstressed. Sanctification is radical humanization. It means doing the "natural" thing spiritually, and the "spiritual" thing naturally. "What a redeemed soul needs," wrote Abraham Kuyper, "is human holiness."[21] Restoration of the image of God to true humanity is God's ultimate purpose for his people. The model and source for this transformation are both found in the humanity of Jesus Christ, the one truly sanctified human.

It is in this context that the thorny issue of the relationship between sanctification and self-image should be discussed. How we view ourselves has an immense impact on the style of our sanctification. Here, the Reformed perspective prevents us from falling into a common trap in discussions of self-image: reductionism and simplification, which invariably result either in what is often disparagingly referred to as worm theology ("Would he devote that sacred head *for such a worm as I?*"), or alternatively in little more than an ego-trip ("God loves me the way I am—period").

The truth of the matter is that now as a Christian I must see myself from two perspectives and say two contrasting things about my life: in myself there dwells no good thing by my own creation or nature (Rom 7:18); and in Christ I have been cleansed, justified and sanctified so that in me glorification has begun (1 Cor 6:11). Even in final glory, presumably, part of the cause of our praise of Christ will be that we are capable of distinguishing between what we have become because of Christ and what we would have become of ourselves. (The Lamb is forever worthy of praise not only because of his eternal divine person, but because he shed his blood to redeem humanity [Rev 5:9].)

The New Testament will not allow us to reduce these two polarities to a common denominator. We must say both: God has given me a new identity with a glorious destiny; in myself I am utterly defiled and deserve only death. I belong to a time when the present evil age and the future glory overlap. I must therefore see myself from two perspectives. Miss this and we miss the biblical doctrine of sanctification, for the Christian's self-image is not properly viewed binocularly, reducing two different perspectives to one, but microscopically, by viewing the variety of activity involved in growth in holiness.

The Means of Sanctification

It should now be clear that in Reformed theology sanctification is by no means a mystical experience in which holiness is ours effortlessly. God gives increase in holiness by engaging our minds, wills, emotions and actions. We are involved in the process. That is why biblical teaching on sanctification appears in both the indicative ("I the Lord sanctify you") and the imperative ("sanctify yourselves this day").

Here we should be careful not to be misled by wrong deductions drawn from biblical metaphors. In some expositions of sanctification, for example, the phrase "the fruit of the Spirit" or the analogy of the vine and the branches (Gal 5:22; Jn 15:1-8) are taken to suggest that

Christian graces grow effortlessly. Indeed, in such teaching effort is sometimes seen as a hindrance to sanctification. Christians are exhorted rather to "let go, and let God have his wonderful way." Similarly, the Christian is encouraged to sing:

> Buried with Christ and raised with him too;
> What is there left for me to do?
> Simply to cease from struggling and strife,
> Simply to walk in newness of life,
> Glory be to God!

But at best this is confusing. At worst the metaphor loses all contact with the control center of the rest of Scripture and goes into an orbit of its own, seriously distorting apostolic teaching. It rends asunder what God has joined together: indicative and imperative; Christ's work and our response of faith; God's grace and our duty.

Reformed teaching on sanctification has focused attention on four areas in which the grace and duties of sanctification coincide. Together, these constitute "means of grace."

The Word

The Word of God is the principal means. It is to be hidden in our hearts as the preservative from sin (Ps 119:11), and those who keep its precepts know the liberty of God's children (v. 45). God's Word is the instrument of both the initial cleansing which takes place in regeneration (Jn 15:3) and the sanctification which continues through the whole Christian life ("Sanctify them by the truth; your word is truth" [Jn 17:17]).

God uses Scripture. It is the "sword of the Spirit" (Eph 6:17). By it our lives are transformed. It is God-breathed for this very purpose, equipping us through its "teaching, rebuking, correcting and training in righteousness" (2 Tim 3:16). It has the power to instruct the mind, introduce clear thinking, inform the conscience and conform us to God's will. At the same time, we are to grab hold of the sword of the Spirit; we have "purified [ourselves] by obeying the truth" (1 Pet 1:22); *we* are to abide in Christ by letting his Word take up residence in our lives (Jn 15:7).

This is why, in Reformed theology, the law of God is seen to play such an important role in sanctification. Its three functions or uses are well known: to convict of sin, to restrain evildoers and to instruct believers. A distinctive feature of Reformed theology is that the third use is seen to be the central one:

> The third and principal use, which pertains more closely to the proper purpose of the law, finds its place among believers in whose hearts the Spirit of God already lives and reigns. For even though they have the law written and engraved upon their hearts by the finger of God [Jer. 31:33; Heb. 10:16], that is, have been so moved and quickened through the directing of the Spirit that they long to obey God, they still profit by the law.[23]

Is this legalism? Legalism means *either* seeking salvation on the basis of obedience to the law *or* believing that every detail of life is covered specifically by some law. But neither of these positions was ever mandated in Scripture, even during the epoch when the Mosaic Law governed life in considerable detail.

God's law expresses what he intended humanity to be when he made us as his image. That is why so many of the commandments in Exodus 20 can readily be traced back to the ordinances of creation in Genesis 1—3. Further, Jesus himself expounds the continuing relevance of the law in the Sermon on the Mount (Mt 5:17-48) and the gospel he proclaimed gave rise to his "new command" (Jn 13:34; 15:9-17).

For this reason sanctification in the New Testament involves conformity to the moral law, for Christ "condemned sin in sinful man, in order that the righteous requirements of the law might be fully met in us, who do not live according to the sinful nature but according to the Spirit" (Rom 8:3-4). Rather than contradict law, love is its fulfillment (Rom 13:8-10). Consequently, the law of God remains the standard of holiness for the New Testament believer. But now (in contrast to what may have been true before becoming a Christian) believers endeavor to fulfill the law, not in order to be justified but because they have already been justified, not in the flesh but in the Spirit, not out of merit-seeking but out of the response of faith which works by love.

This emphasis on Scripture as a means of sanctification also helps to explain why Reformed theology has placed such an emphasis on preaching as an instrument in sanctification. Expository preaching which engaged the minds of the congregation as hearers (in contrast to elaborate liturgy at which the congregation were spectators) was a leading characteristic of all the mainstream reformers, not least of which was Martin Luther; but it has been in the Reformed churches that this emphasis has been most marked.

Calvin preached several times each week in Geneva, patiently expounding book after book of Scripture. (Indeed, when he returned to the pulpit of St. Peter's church after a period of forced exile, he simply carried on expounding from the point at which he had left off![24]) In one form or another such in-depth preaching characterized the later Puritans and other Reformed pastors such as Jonathan Edwards.

What is so striking about their sermons, however, is that they covered the whole Word of God and did not limit their preaching either to a few "evangelistic" texts or necessarily to evangelistically oriented messages. Compare many of these older sermons with much evangelical preaching today and one is struck by the contrast. How much doctrine they taught from Scripture! They believed that the whole Bible was given to make whole Christians.

This emphasis on preaching is grounded in the conviction that God works through it to sanctify his people. Because God's Word of grace "can build you up and give you an inheritance among all those who are sanctified" (Acts 20:32) and is useful for "teaching, rebuking, correcting and training in righteousness" (2 Tim 3:16), it is to be preached (2 Tim 4:2).

For this purpose God has given gifts to his church to help us to reach full maturity (Eph 4:11-16). It is interesting in this context that those Paul mentions are all (apparently) ministries of the Word. It is equally interesting that the Ephesian church (which received this instruction along with other congregations) had firsthand experience of what Paul had in mind. He had taught them daily in the lecture hall of Tyrannus and from house to house (Acts 20:20). This went on for three years, Luke notes. Indeed, one tradition records that these meetings lasted for five hours each day![25]

This in no way denigrates the private reading and study of Scripture (a phenomenon simply not possible for the first Christians, since even if they had been able to collect the entire canon of the New Testament, the materials required for one copy would have cost a year's wages). But it does emphasize the strategic role which public exposition of Scripture can play in the life of the church, and also the premium which

Scripture places on the mind and its activity in sanctification. It is by the *renewal* of the mind that we are transformed by the Spirit, as we reflect (or contemplate) the glory of the Lord in Scripture (Rom 12:1-2; 2 Cor 3:18).

The Providences

The providences of God, not least of which are severe trials and afflictions, are also ordained for the purpose of sanctification. "These afflictions," wrote John Flavel, with the quaintness characteristic of a seventeenth-century divine, "have the same use and end to our souls, that frosty weather hath upon those clothes that are laid and bleaching, they alter the hue and make them white."[26]

This is confirmed by biblical biography and explicit testimony. In most of the key figures in redemptive history we can trace the way in which God's providences molded their characters. What people or devils intend for evil, God intends for good (Gen 50:20). Affliction serves as a divine beacon for those who are going astray (Ps 119:67).

We have already discussed this theme from another point of view in considering the external dimension of mortification. That discussion should serve to remind us that providence yields sanctification only as it is experienced in union with Christ. Only to those who love God and are called (into union with Christ) according to his purpose, do all things work together for good (Rom 8:28). This is because in his foreknowledge, God has predestined his people to be conformed to the image of Christ (Rom 8:29). Because this is the end in view in all the circumstances of life, believers can respond to them positively, knowing that the Spirit of God is employing them in his transforming ministry. In providence, then, the believer looks for God's handiwork and submits to God's severe mercies. Indeed, says Calvin, united to Christ, "the church of Christ has been from the beginning so constituted that the Cross has been the way to victory and death the way to life."[27] United to Christ, we understand providences in these terms: "Just as the sufferings of Christ flow over into our lives, so also through Christ our comfort overflows" (2 Cor 1:5).

The Fellowship of the Church

The fellowship of the church is the context in which sanctification matures, and in this sense is also a means for its development. For sanctification involves our attitudes and actions in relation to others. The love which is the heart of imitation of Christ (compare to 1 Cor 13) cannot be isolationist; the death of our inordinate love of self is tested therefore in fellowship. This is the thrust of Paul's exposition of true sanctification in the context of weak and strong sharing the same fellowship: "We who are strong ought to bear with the failings of the weak and not to please ourselves. Each of us should please his neighbor for his good, to build him up. For even Christ did not please himself" (Rom 15:1-3).

Reformed theology sees the church as a preaching and suffering community. By these means it is sanctified, is thus transformed into Christ's likeness and so bears witness in the world. But several other elements mark the true church. Included among them are the fact that the church is a caring and praying community. These elements in its life are also helps for our sanctification.

The church is a fellowship of pastoral care. Explicit directions are given to those who have specific gifts (Rom 12:3-8, for example). But exhortation is also given to the whole church to exercise a pastoral ministry: "To each one the manifestation of the Spirit is given *for the common good*" (1 Cor 12:7, emphasis mine). It is "as each part does its work" that the whole body in Christ "grows and builds itself up in love" (Eph 4:16). We "teach and admonish one another with all wisdom" (Col 3:16). The New Testament letters illustrate this regularly, both with extended exposition and with what we might call apostolic one-liners—simple epigrams which are aimed at the mutual encouragement of holy living. If we bear in mind that the recipients of the "practical" segments in Paul's letters are addressed in the second person plural, his intended impact will become clear. His logic is that these things are to be true of all of you as a church and therefore of each of you as individuals.

By contrast, our logic in the twentieth century has tended to be that once these things are true of me individually, and I can gather enough individuals like myself around me, then they will be true of the church. We move from the individual to the corporate, the microcosm to the macrocosm. Paul's teaching moves in the opposite direction. Once that is grasped, the necessity of church association for true sanctification becomes self-evident.

The church is also a community of prayer. Again the sheer weight of the prayers which permeate the apostolic writings confirm this and shame the contemporary church for its mistaken assumption that sanctification can be produced prayerlessly. This is a theme which requires extended treatment beyond the scope of this essay.[28] Here it is sufficient to mention it for the sake of completeness in expressing the Reformed standing on sanctification.

The Sacraments

Finally, it should be noted that in Reformed theology, the sacraments play an important role in sanctification. How they do was a major bone of contention at the time of the Reformation and remains so today, and cannot be expounded in detail here. Simply expressed, in Reformed teaching, the sacraments are communicative signs. They point us away from ourselves to Christ; but they also are a visible, tangible means by which he communicates with us and we with him. They display his grace and our union and communion with him in it. They mark off and remind us of the distinction between the church and the world (Rom 6:1-4; 1 Cor 10:16, 21). In doing so, they provide incentives to Christlikeness and sanctification.

The sacraments can never be separated from the Word of God. Nor do the sacraments provide sanctifying grace from Christ which is not available to us in the message of the Scriptures. It is the same grace we receive, because it is the same Christ who is held out to us. Both Scripture and sacraments point to the same Lord. But, as Robert Bruce so well expressed it, while we do not get a better Christ in the sacraments than we do in the Word, there are times when we get Christ better.[29] In the words of Horatius Bonar's communion hymn which so well represents the Reformed approach to the Lord's Table,

Here O my Lord, I see Thee face to face;
Here would I touch and handle things unseen,
Here grasp with firmer hand the eternal grace,
And all my weariness upon Thee lean.

The sacraments are helps to sanctification precisely because they are means to a fresh realization of our union and communion with Christ. They point us back to its foundation and forward to its consummation in glory (as we have been buried with Christ in baptism, we will be raised with him in resurrection; as we commune with the crucified and risen Christ, we also proclaim him until he comes again). Here we are brought back to the foundation on which the Reformed understanding of sanctification rests: union with Christ. We are baptized into him and share in the virtue of his death and resurrection; as we eat the bread and drink the wine, we are able to say, because of that union, "I have been crucified with Christ and I no longer live, but Christ lives in me. The life I live in the body, I live by faith in the Son of God, who loved me and gave himself for me" (Gal 2:20).

Sanctification is simply the outworking of this communion. We become like those with whom we have the closest communion; and in Reformed theology, sanctification means becoming like Christ.

Notes

[1]Such statements inevitably involve a subjective reading of history, but note the words of I. H. Marshall (my own esteemed New Testament teacher, and himself a Wesleyan Methodist) to the same effect: "within conservative evangelicalism the dominant school of thought is Calvinism." *Kept by the Power of God* (Minneapolis, Minn.: Bethany, 1975), preface.

[2]First published in 1536 and revised constantly, the work known in English as the *Institutes* is a translation of the final Latin edition of 1559.

[3]For Calvin "piety" did not mean what is sometimes connoted by "pietism" today, that is, a separation of life into sacred and secular and a withdrawing from the latter. Rather, Calvin states, "I call 'piety' that reverence joined with love of God which the knowledge of his benefits induces" *(Institutes* 1.2.1). For Calvin this governs the whole of life.

[4]David Clarkson, "A Funeral Sermon on the Much Lamented Death of the Late Reverend and Learned Divine John Owen, D.D." (London, 1720). Clarkson was at one time Owen's assistant and was a leading seventeenth-century theologian in his own right.

[5]Calvin *Institutes* 3.1.1.

[6]"The noun *archēgos* is difficult to translate satisfactorily. It signifies one who is both the source or initiator and the leader (*archē* plus *agō*), one who first takes action and then brings on those on whose behalf he has acted to the intended goal." P. E. Hughes, *Commentary on the Epistle to the Hebrews* (Grand Rapids, Mich.: Eerdmans, 1977), p. 100, fn. 88.

[7]Calvin *Institutes* 2.16.19.

[8]"Of Sanctification," *The [Westminster] Confession of Faith* 13.1.

[9]The classic exposition of this view is found in Robert Haldane, *The Epistle to the Romans* (reprinted, London, 1966). He has been followed by many exegetes since, including in recent times C. E. B. Cranfield, *A Critical and Exegetical Commentary on the Epistle to the Romans,* 2 vols. (Edinburgh: T. & T. Clark, vol. 1, 1975; vol. 2, 1979).

[10]See John Murray, *The Epistle to the Romans,* 2 vols. (Grand Rapids, Mich.: Eerdmans vol. 1, 1959; vol. 2, 1960), 1:222; also Ernst Kasemann, *Commentary on Romans,* trans.

and ed. G. W. Bromiley (Grand Rapids, Mich.: Eerdmans, 1980): "Paul's concern is not with guilt, but with the power of sin" (p. 170).

C. E. B. Cranfield's exposition at this point fails to take account of the entire context of Paul's teaching in Romans 6. He says that "free from sin" (Rom 6:7) "must clearly mean 'has been justified from sin' rather than 'has been freed from sin' . . . since, while . . . the Christian is no longer the completely helpless and unresisting slave of sin, he is not in this life actually free from sin" (1:311).

Cranfield shares with other exegetes the nervousness that if Paul affirmed Christians are free from sin he would be guilty of the very perfectionism the New Testament elsewhere denies (compare to 1 Jn 1:5-10) and also from the continual warfare in which the Christian is engaged (Gal 5:17). But the perspective from which Paul speaks in Romans 5—7 is one in which he sees sin as a tyrant-king from whose reign (not presence or even influence) Christ delivers the Christian. Curiously, on 6:18, Cranfield states this without showing his earlier reservations: "They have already been set free from sin in the sense that they have been transferred from the possession of sin to the possession of a new master and so are now in a position to resist sin's controlling hold upon them" (1:325).

[11]Paul's relative pronoun here *(hoitines)* appears to be equivalent to the Latin *quippe qui* ("seeing that"). The sense is "which by its very nature." Compare to H. G. C. Moule, *Idiom Book of the New Testament* (Cambridge: Cambridge University Press, 1960), pp. 123-25.

[12]Compare to G. Kittel and G. Friedrich, *Theological Dictionary of the New Testament*, vol. 7, trans. G. W. Bromiley (Grand Rapids, Mich.: Eerdmans, 1964-76), p. 786, for the view that "the basic meaning is 'native.' "

[13]John Murray, *Principles of Conduct* (Grand Rapids, Mich.: Eerdmans, 1957), p. 205.

[14]John Owen, *Works*, ed. W. H. Goold, 24 vols., (Carlisle, Pa.: Banner of Truth, 1980), 7:517.

[15]Calvin *Institutes* 1.18.1.

[16]Outstanding examples of these are William Gurnall, *The Christian in Complete Armour* (London, 1662-65) and Thomas Brooks, *Precious Remedies Against Satan's Devices* (London, 1652). For a modern exposition in the same tradition, see D. Martyn Lloyd-Jones, *The Christian Warfare* (Edinburgh, 1976) and *The Christian Soldier* (Carlisle, Pa.: Banner of Truth, 1977).

[17]In recent decades the weight of opinion, under the powerful influence of European scholarship, largely has been committed to some form of the view that Romans 7:14-25 does not describe Paul's personal Christian experience. It is of interest to note the relatively recent expressions of commitment to the "traditional" Reformed view on the part of three leading English-speaking scholars: J. I. Packer, "The Wretched Man in Romans 7," *Studia Evangelica* 2, pp. 621-27; J. D. G. Dunn, "Rom 7:14-25 in the Theology of Paul," *Theologische Zeitschrift* 31 (1975), pp. 257-73; Cranfield, *Commentary on Romans*.

[18]G. C. Berkouwer, *Faith and Sanctification*, vol. 1, Studies in Dogmatics: Theology (Grand Rapids, Mich.: Eerdmans, 1952), p. 60.

[19]Such is the force of Rom 7:25 that many modern commentators find themselves driven to conclude either that the verse is misplaced, and originally came after verse 23, or that it is a scribal gloss. But, as Kasemann (who adopts the latter position) recognizes, this is "against the whole textual tradition."

[20]Owen, *Works*, 6:14.

[21]Louis Berkhof, *Systematic Theology* (Grand Rapids, Mich.: Eerdmans, 1978), p. 451.

[22]Abraham Kuyper, *The Work of the Holy Spirit,* trans. H. De Vries (New York: Funk & Wagnalls, 1900), p. 461.

[23]Calvin *Institutes* 2.7.12.

[24]Various preaching programs marked Calvin's extended ministry in Geneva, involving him in preaching every day on alternate weeks and twice on Sundays. This marked a decrease in his preaching load from an earlier period of ministry!

[25]The Western text adds to Acts 19:9 that Paul taught in the lecture hall of Tyrannus, "from the fifth to the tenth hour" (from 11 A.M. to 4 P.M.), on which F. F. Bruce comments, "A very reasonable guess, if guess it be. Tyrannus no doubt gave his lectures before 11 a.m. at which hour public life in Ionian cities, as elsewhere, regularly ended," *The Acts of the Apostles* (Grand Rapids, Mich.: Eerdmans, 1953), p. 356.

[26]John Flavel, *Works* (Carlisle, Pa.: Banner of Truth, 1820), 4:407.

[27]John Calvin, *The Epistle of Paul to the Hebrews, The Epistles of Peter,* ed. D. W. Torrance, trans. W. B. Johnston (Edinburgh, 1963), p. 240.

[28]I have suggested a Reformed or covenantal approach to prayer in "Prayer—A Covenant Work," *Banner of Truth Magazine* 137 (1975), pp. 23ff.

[32]Robert Bruce, *The Mystery of the Lord's Supper,* trans. and ed. Thomas F. Torrance (Richmond, Va.: John Knox Press, 1958).

A Lutheran Response
Gerhard O. Forde

T
O BEGIN WITH, I'LL SAY THAT I AM HIGHLY APPRECIATIVE OF
Mr. Ferguson's excellent presentation of the Reformed view.
I can see many points of similarity and complementarity with
what I attempted in my essay. The careful exegetical work is especially
commendable. I am particularly impressed by the fact that he makes
Romans 6 so absolutely central and crucial for the evangelical understanding of sanctification. I am in basic agreement with him in his
exegesis of that passage and the treatment of sanctification in terms of
the death of the old and the life of the new in Christ. This is the heart
of the matter. The manner in which we understand and express ourselves in light of this death and new life will virtually determine our
grasp of sanctification.

That we have to do with death and life, however, means, as I tried
to indicate, that speaking of sanctification can be a very subtle and even
dangerous business. I think that most of our talk about it represents
the bad conscience of the old (moral or immoral!) being who has not
really been put to death and so is worried because salvation as a free
gift seems too easy and cheap. Since the old being has not died, the
law is still in some sense in effect, and so sanctification becomes merely
a repair job on the old, a progress according to the law, a transition

from vice to virtue for the continuously existing being. To avoid the charge of "cheap grace" we talk very seriously and grandly about sanctification. The result, however, is only that a good deal of cheap talk replaces the cheap grace.

Consequently I watch very closely the way in which we talk about sanctification. To begin with, the problem lies in what we think such talk is supposed to accomplish. There is quite a difference between adequately describing sanctification and actually fostering or producing it. The *description* may be quite true, nice, accurate or even enticing, but it may be accompanied with an inadequate understanding of how to effect such things evangelically. We can end by preaching a description of the sanctified life but doing little or nothing to bring it about.

Preaching a description is deadly and usually counterproductive. It is like yelling so loudly at your children to go to sleep that you only keep them awake. You have to learn to sing lullabies. Or it is like telling your beloved that "love means thus-and-so, and if you really love me then you would do thus-and-so." While the description may be true, it's not likely to work. More often it will have the opposite effect. Instead one has to learn to say, "I love you, no matter what."

"Faith without works is dead," we are reminded. Quite true. But then what follows is usually some long and dreary description of works and what we should be about, as though the way to revive a dead faith were by putting up a good-works front. If the faith is dead, it is the faith that must be revived. No amount of works will do it. Whatever may be accomplished by such hollering about works—though it may even be considerable—does not really qualify as sanctification, that is, true holiness.

All of this is not to say that Mr. Ferguson's fine essay can be faulted for overtly or grossly going astray in this regard, but it is to indicate the angle from which my response here, as well as to the other essays, is aimed. By and large the *description* of sanctification is helpful, exegetically sound and exciting. Indeed, centering on Romans 6 is crucial. Ferguson's exegesis is convincing. The insistence that true sanctification flows from union with the crucified and risen Christ is vital. Particularly apt is the insistence that our dying and rising with Christ is not a project to be accomplished by some "process" or other, but that it is over—we *have* died. Furthermore, the judgment that "We miss the radical nature of Paul's teaching here to our great loss" can only be underscored. All of this means that true sanctification is what flows from the new life. Ferguson says as much when he states that "Sanctification is therefore the consistent practical outworking of what it means to belong to the new creation in Christ."

But I suppose that is just the neuralgic point. What does it mean for us to belong to the new creation in Christ for the time being? What does it mean to be a new being by faith and yet still live in the old age? The temptation in our talk of sanctification is to get nervous and forget, miss or obscure this eschatological dialectic. This occurs when we begin to preach our descriptions as though they were actually maps and motivational influences to power the new life. Christian theologians have consistently criticized the Greek philosophers for saying that knowledge of or exhortation to the good does not necessarily result in doing the good, but then those same theologians turn about and do much the same in their talk of sanctification.

Ferguson tends in this direction in the sections of his essay dealing with the "outworking" of the doctrine and "The Means of Sanctification." That is particularly true in the negative comments about sanctification as a "mystical experience in which holiness is ours effortlessly," and in the move to talk about the "third" use of the law in the Reformed perspective. Then, a rather dense Puritan fog begins to roll in and the radical nature of Paul's teaching about death and life, previously so carefully developed and affirmed, begins to fade from sight. The problem here is extremely subtle, and so one must proceed with caution so as to isolate the difficulty. The basic difficulty with a view of sanctification depending heavily on instruction and a "third use of the law" is that it obscures the eschatological vision and hope of the Christian. It reintroduces the law in a supposed "third" use *after* the advent of the new. It overplays the role of the law in sanctification.

There need be no pointless argument about whether we as the persons we are now, even as believing Christians, still need to have the law preached to us. Indeed we do. The eschatological question, however, is whether we need this *as Christians,* as new beings, or rather because we are *not yet* Christians in the full eschatological sense. If it is the case that we have need of the preaching of the law, then surely it must be the latter, and for the same reason that the rest of humankind needs it. In other words, we need the law for the same reason as the non-Christian, in its first two uses: to restrain evil and convict us of sin. If we do not know what to do, then there is the law and wholesome instruction from the tradition and the general fund of human wisdom to inform us.

But the eschatological hope that fires the Christian is precisely that the law is limited to this age; that it has its end (both *telos* and *finis*) in Christ; that there will come a day when there shall be no law, no Temple; when we shall know as we are known; when the good will be done freely and spontaneously—yes, even effortlessly!—for its own sake; and even God will no longer be "needed," but simply enjoyed. We must hold out for this eschatological vision because it is just that, *not* the law, that is the driving force behind true sanctification. Paul knew that. It was precisely for that reason that he insisted so strongly on the eschatological truth: you *have* died, and so shall have life! You are not of the flesh but of the Spirit! If there is no light at the end of the tunnel, then the darkness in which we live is the darkness of the tomb. I believe that this may be the reason why so much of our talk, our endless description, of sanctification bears so little fruit. It has no "end." The joy, the *hilaritas,* of faith is dampened by our nervousness about the law. We spend so much time and effort talking *about* love that we never get around to saying "I love you."

Consequently I do not think that easy or casual dismissals of the spontaneity of faith (what Ferguson terms "effortlessness" in acquiring holiness) do us much good. Of course we all know that we fail to do the good spontaneously much of the time. And we all know that we need instruction and exhortation. But this tragedy is due to the absence of holiness; it does not cause it. If righteousness comes by faith alone, and is bestowed on us for Christ's sake alone, then holiness too—true holiness—comes the same way. It is a gift. We cannot drive a wedge between justification and sanctification at this point. The Reformers (particularly Luther) were not being simply naive, as is often charged, when they celebrated the spontaneity and the *hilaritas* of faith. They knew the foibles and failings of humans better than any, and they certainly recognized the need for continued application of the law. Luther especially knew that the law does not produce holiness, not even in its "third use." The gospel is the source of holiness, the power of

Forde paints a picture that obeid need to the law sanctifys us. This is what he says the reformed view B.

God unto salvation. It is not the law.

Losing sight of the eschatological vision not only obscures the gospel, however; it also disarms the law. When one speaks of a "third use" as a gentle guide for the Christian, several things happen. First, one tends to domesticate the law. One tries to make a tame house-pet out of the raging lion. It can't really be done. That is why, in spite of protestations, the law takes over and legalism reigns. Once you let the lion into the eschatological "house," it can't be so easily controlled!

Second, one mistakes just who is the subject of the use. One tends to think that Christians have now progressed to a stage where *they* use the law in a third way. But there is a little hubris in that. After all, the law is God's, and God is the user. We do not preside over that, and so cannot domesticate it. Only Christ, grasped in faith, is the end of the law, not the Christian and certainly not Christian theology or ethics.

Finally, talk of a "third use" mistakes the relation of the Christian in this present age to the law. The very idea of a "third use" presupposes a certain understanding of Christian conversion in which Christians have supposedly passed a point in time beyond which they can now come under a use of the law quite different from all the rest of the people of the world. Again, there seems a little hubris in that. Precisely because Christians have been caught by the eschatological vision, they should not think that way. And because we see by faith the light at the end of the tunnel, and how much we fall short of that, we should have no illusions about ourselves. Rather we should realize our solidarity with the rest of humankind in sin and how much we need still to hear the law.

To be sure, because of this faith, the Christian does know something the non-Christian does not know. But what the Christian knows by faith is that the law does have its *end* in Christ. What the Christian knows is not a different *use* of the law, but just the difference between law and gospel, and thus what law is for. Precisely because of the eschatological vision, faith does not abolish the law, but establishes it. *Perspectiv PA* When that vision is lost, when Christ is not the end of the law, we take steps to end it or tame it ourselves. But that only means theological disaster—both for the gospel and the law. Where the gospel is not the end of the law, the law remains the way of salvation and the gospel is reduced to the status of a "help" in doing the law. Consequently the law too must be reduced to manageable proportions by some sort of casuistry.

To sum up my response: The description of sanctification in Ferguson's essay is accurate and compelling. The implementation, however, is less convincing. If it is true that sanctification is the outworking of the fact that we have died and been made new in Christ, we should then pay more attention to the sort of thing Paul says following Romans 6—especially Romans 8!

A Wesleyan Response
Laurence W. Wood

ERGUSON'S DEFINITION OF SANCTIFICATION HAS A TWOFOLD EM-
phasis. On the one hand, it involves our being in Christ. On
the other hand, it means our being infused with righteousness
through "union with Christ." What we are in Christ and what we
become in actuality through our relationship to Christ are closely interrelated aspects of sanctification.

While sanctification has certainly been an important doctrine within
both the Reformed and Wesleyan traditions, there are some significant
differences of emphasis in their respective understandings, even though
they share a broad area of agreement.

First, Wesley emphasizes that the doctrine of sanctification is a perfect love for God. Holy love is characteristic of God's nature, and this
love has been poured forth in our hearts through the Holy Spirit (Rom
5:5). This ethical-relational dimension of sanctification is primary. Not
external performance and behavior but the intent of the heart is decisive. Psychological maladjustments and inappropriate behavior resulting from mistaken judgments are compatible with the experience of
perfect love—although the difference between intention and performance should not be considerable!

Second, Ferguson stresses performance and moral imperatives as decisive aspects of sanctification. Hence he refers to sanctification largely in terms of "growth" toward the ideal of holiness. In this respect, it would seem that the legal fulfilling of the divine law is the primary meaning of sanctification for Ferguson. To be sure, Ferguson wants to avoid a legalism-moralism, but to focus on the meaning of sanctification primarily in terms of performance instead of on the relational dimension of love makes it difficult to avoid Puritanical and moralistic attitudes. In this respect, the Reformed view typically begins with a heavy emphasis on the sovereignty of God, whose decrees tell us how we should *then* live (to paraphrase Ferguson and Schaeffer). The Wesleyan tradition, while affirming the sovereignty of God, emphasizes his nature as holy love. God's desire for us is to enter into an intimacy of friendship (Jn 15:15) with him through Christ. Performance is certainly an indication of the depth of our friendship with God, but the sincerity of the relationship is the decisive thing.

Third, Wesley had an affirming attitude about the created world—even though it is fallen. Every person is a sinner by birth and by choice. Yet by the prevenient grace of God a measure of goodness has been restored to the fallen world. Total depravity in the sense that evil has negatively influenced every aspect of the created world extensively—though not intensively—is an essential part of Wesley's teaching. But because of the prevenient and redeeming grace of God in Jesus Christ it is still possible to love God in this world with all one's heart. This experience of perfect love is the essence of righteousness. Hence John says that we can love God perfectly and that we can be righteous in this world even as Christ is righteous (1 Jn 4:17). Again, the focus of righteousness is on the ethical-relational dimension of love, not on a legal performance of commandments.

Ferguson argues, as does Calvin, that as long as we are in this physical body it is impossible to experience a perfection of love. Ferguson says those who interpret Paul's words, "dead to sin," "the death of the old man," "freedom from sin" as if he really meant this literally and actually are "abusing" Paul's thoughts and intention. For Wesley, these phrases mean one thing—we love God with all the heart. Wesley was not at all assuming that these terms had anything to do with perfect performance. The Wesleyan tradition interprets Paul's statements about the meaning of "freedom from sin" ethically and relationally. The whole tenor of his writings is that the gospel of grace truly regenerates and truly sanctifies. Even though we are living in a fallen world we can enter this relationship with Christ. As contemporary New Testament scholarship widely acknowledges, Paul's concern is with the ethical level of living; he calls for us to be holy in heart and life and leaves no place for voluntary and known sin in the life of the believer. In Romans 7:14, Paul describes himself as "sold under sin." Here Paul is surely speaking (rhetorically) in the historical present tense for dramatic purposes, and hence goes on to show that Christ truly liberates from this dominion of sin.

Skevington Wood labels Romans 8 as "Paul's Pentecost." Romans 8 is the stage beyond Romans 7, for the life of the Spirit has set him free from sin (Rom 8:2). A legalistic definition of sin is surely not what Paul has in mind, but rather the context suggests an ethical-relational understanding. So long as a legalistic definition dominates one's understanding, the New Testament ethical use of sin is overlooked. In an overwhelming number of instances in the New Testament, use of the verb form *to sin* carries with it the idea of willful and known sin. Only a handful of references to sinning can be defined in a legal sense. Without careful contextual reading of Paul's use of *sin,* one is left puzzled about what Paul means to live without sin. Except for a very few instances in the New Testament, the definition of the act of sinning (the verb form *to sin*) assumes a voluntary transgression of the known law of God. Also, the singular noun form of *sin* normally means *inherited depravity,* an abstract theological expression which means that from birth one's life is characterized by sinful pride—that is, a love centered in on oneself.

A legal definition is that *sin* is any deviation from the will of God, voluntary or involuntary. To be sure, the legal definition is valid. Whether intentional or not, any failure to fulfill the will of God is sinning, and everyone sins involuntarily, even the believer made perfect in love. This is why Wesley insisted that Christian perfection is not a sinless perfection. On the other hand, there is an ethical distinction to be made between intentional and unintentional sinning. Hence the assumption throughout the New Testament about living without sinning employs the ethical meaning of sinning. Otherwise the biblical condemnation and judgment pronounced on those who sin and the

incompatibility of loving God and sinning (1 Jn 3:9) are unintelligible.
Grace and sin are incompatible (Rom 6:1). Paul counsels believers to
be understanding with the "failings of the weak" (Rom 15:1), but he
tells Timothy to rebuke those who sin (1 Tim 5:20). Involuntary sin
or mistakes are compatible with perfect love, but not voluntary sin.
Despite maladjustments and involuntary sins, one can still simultaneously be filled with the love of God.

To be justified by faith is to experience forgiveness of sins and to
be enabled through the power of the Spirit to live a life of victory over
sinning. In this justifying moment, sanctification begins because *sin*
(the singular noun form refers to the original condition of the heart
from birth) no longer dominates a person's life. "Entire" sanctification
is only a further stage along the always-growing process of the sanctified life, and this experience can only follow the initial state of the
new birth (in which one's heart is "cleansed" from inward sinfulness).
This means that one is free to truly love God with one's whole heart.
In this "deeper life" of the Spirit, one engages in significant spiritual
growth as one's pure love for God increases even more and more.

If one is freed from sin (inherited depravity), can one really commit
any more acts of sin? Obviously Adam was sinless in a way not possible
even for the sanctified person today; yet he was tempted and did sin.
The temptation to sin does not simply arise from "an inborn tendency
of sinfulness," but rather this inner sinful condition predisposes one
to a susceptibility to sinning. To be free from sin is a metaphorical way
of saying that one's heart is fully devoted to God's will.

Finally, Ferguson shows exegetically that the disciples were genuinely converted before Pentecost. In their case, he allows there was a
difference between their initial conversion and their "baptism with the
Spirit." However, this experiential distinction is allegedly unique to the
disciples because they were conditioned in time by the flow of these
salvation events. A Wesleyan view does not hold to a rigid notion of
time in such a purely sequential way. It may be that the experience of
some believers on the continuum of salvation history are pre-Abraham-
ic; others are pre-Mosaic; some are pre-Pentecostal; some are Pentecostal Christians. The quality of one's Christian life is measured in
terms of where one is participating in the timeline of salvation history.

Implicit in Wesley and explicit in John Fletcher (Wesley's closest friend and personally chosen successor as leader of the Methodists) is the identification of the fullness of the Spirit with the experience of perfect love for God. For Pentecost made possible the realization of a perfect love for God that the Old Testament had promised would be available at the time of the eschatological outpouring of the Spirit (Deut 30:6; Jer 24:7; Ezek 11:19; 36:26-27). The several instances in Acts where there is a distinction in time between believers' repentance and initial faith in Christ and a subsequent reception of the Pentecostal Spirit implies that this pattern is typical in the life of believers. In this respect, Easter comes before Pentecost in salvation history, and likewise in the saving history of individual believers. Hence a real distinction exists logically and temporally between Easter and Pentecost. To be sure, the time distinction lies on a continuum. That is, one's personal Easter and Pentecost are closely interrelated along a timeline. They are decisive events in the personal history of the believer, but as such they are events continuously relived and updated daily. Experiencing the perfect love of Christ is not a static state of grace, but is always a dialectical *becoming* of a reality that has happened and continues to happen as we grow in grace!

A Pentecostal Response
Russell P. Spittler

IT IS EASY FOR A MEMBER OF THE ASSEMBLIES OF GOD QUICKLY TO say "Amen" to Ferguson's overall conception of sanctification. That's because this variety of Pentecostalism is a step removed from the more Wesleyan moorings that characterized the early Pentecostals. William Durham's teachings on the "finished work of Christ" profoundly affected those leaders who formed the Assemblies of God. The impact of Durham's teaching was to make sanctification not a "second blessing" (as the Wesleyans and the Wesleyan Pentecostals believed), but rather as coterminous with salvation—beginning at conversion and concluding at the death of the believer. The Open Bible Standard Churches and the International Church of the Foursquare Gospel are two other examples of denominations that reflect the influence of the Reformed church.

The Reformed professor's sentences easily become the Pentecostal's own: "It is by the ministry of God's Spirit and by the exercise of the believer's faith" that Christ meets our need. "Faith involves trusting in and resting on the resources of Christ as though they were our own."

But it comes as a surprise to read that the first followers of Jesus, admittedly regenerated before they were baptized in the Holy Spirit, were a separate case—unique because initial. "After the initial period of overlap between the Old and New epochs of redemption, being brought 'into' Christ by faith, regeneration *and* baptism with the Spirit take place simultaneously—a threefold perspective on the one event in which no perspective is simply reducible to either of the other two." Classical Pentecostals draw an opposite conclusion: What happened in the New Testament models what can—and should—happen today. Hence the idea of the subsequence of the baptism in the Holy Spirit emerged even among the Reformed wing of classical Pentecostals.

But the adoption of the Reformed idea of sanctification is by no means universal among classical Pentecostals. Groups like the Pentecostal Holiness Church and the Church of God (Cleveland, Tennessee) emerge with a threefold order of salvation: conversion, sanctification (in the Wesleyan, postconversional, crisis-experience model, resulting in enhanced personal holiness) and then baptism in the Holy Spirit. Reformed Pentecostals in effect merged the second and third of these three.

The Scriptures, preaching of the Word and churchly fellowship would all be seconded by Pentecostals of every variety as the means by which sanctification is effected—even though among the Wesleyan Pentecostals the crisis experience yields a past-tense statement: "I've been sanctified."

But on two of Ferguson's other "means of grace," Pentecostals do not so readily agree. Though trials are viewed as sources of growth, there is little said positively among Pentecostals about the spiritual usefulness of suffering. The neglect rises from the belief in healing universally held among Pentecostals. Suffering suggests failed healing, to oversimplify considerably.

The second hesitance appears with the term "sacraments." Most Pentecostals call them "ordinances." And since both the term "sacraments" and their practice marked the established churches out of which the early Pentecostals came, there is no high doctrine of the sacraments. The highest motive for their practice, for the most part, is "because Jesus told us to do it."

Quite possibly Reformed Pentecostals, as well as charismatics (who don't often mention sanctification), should reconsider the doctrine and practice of sanctification. But among Pentecostals, one risks being heard as calling them to a stricter lifestyle—"holiness" in dress, denied entertainment and restricted ecclesiastical association.

   The dutiful attention to controlling behavior patterns is based on the unpromising assumption that reproducing an effect recaptures its cause. What would emerge if Pentecostal teachers and pastors reconsidered the biblical roots of sanctification and concluded that it begins with the heart and leads to changes in lifestyle? Such a rediscovery of sanctification could very well lead to the recovery of true holiness valued by all who believe.

A Contemplative Response
E. Glenn Hinson

THE REFORMED PERSPECTIVE ON SANCTIFICATION REFLECTS such remarkable affinity with the contemplative tradition that I can say little negative about this lucid and helpful paper. If anything is to be faulted about it, it would be the suggestion that these are "distinctive features" of the Reformed tradition, as if rediscovered there, for they are continuous with the medieval contemplative tradition. The Puritans self-consciously returned to that well in order to effect the "further reformation" and the "holy commonwealth" they sought in England and New England. Let me highlight the agreements and differences and then elaborate on this point.

Medieval contemplatives, many virtually illiterate, will not have stressed Scripture strongly or in quite the same manner as Calvin and his heirs. Contrary to what Protestants sometimes assume, however, they were highly important in the development of the devout and holy life. One of the chief forms of prayer was the *lectio divina*, in which contemplatives sought by deep reflection to hear the Word of God and take it to heart. Those who could not read for themselves relied on hearing and memorizing Scriptures during corporate worship.

Contemplatives would have agreed with the Reformed that "Jesus Christ himself is our sanctification or holiness"; and that sanctification occurs through union with Christ. They drew metaphors from the intimate human relationship of marriage to express all of this and found rich imagery in the Song of Songs to depict their experience. It is amazing (as I have demonstrated in an article entitled "Southern Baptist and Medieval Monastic Spirituality: Surprising Similarities") how many hymns of the Baptist tradition (a wing of the Reformed) replicate the very language of medieval saints like Bernard of Clairvaux and Richard Rolle. A recurrent accent there as here is: it's all of grace, God's grace in Christ.

A critical point at which I think the Reformed tradition comes into closer agreement with the contemplative than does the Lutheran is in the understanding of grace. Grace is not merely God's forgiveness of the sinner, but God himself, the Risen Christ, the Holy Spirit, *transforming* those who have committed themselves to Christ. By yielding ourselves to God, we really can and do become new persons. Contemplatives would heartily endorse Calvin's exhortation "to embrace Christ, not only into righteousness, but also unto sanctification . . . lest through their lame faith they rend Christ in pieces." In neither tradition does this mean sinless perfection—far from it. Rather, it means the Risen Christ gives power to do better, to live free from the dreadful grip of egocentrism and pride. Axiomatic for both traditions is the fact that, given the power of God in Christ, we are no longer slaves of sin but rather servants of God. The new creation works itself out in Christ.

Both traditions view the consequences of sanctification in the same way, using much of the same imagery. Progress in holiness entails pilgrimage and "holy war." Satan and his hosts constantly assail those who strive to be faithful, the believer perhaps more than the unbeliever. Sanctification will entail mortification, that is, putting the old self to death. Thus the cross is central. We are united with Christ in dying so as to be united with him in overcoming sin and death. Our way to achieve this is to follow Christ, walk in his footsteps or imitate him— the theme of the great fourteenth-century classic *The Imitation of Christ*. Both traditions tend to trip over "worm theology," but in more reflective writings they hold in balance human propensity for sin and unworthiness, and divine love that turns sinners into saints.

The Reformed and the contemplative traditions have relied on similar means of sanctification: the Word of God in Scriptures and sermon, experiences in the depths, the fellowship of believers, prayer and the sacraments. Ferguson's article seriously underemphasizes the role of prayer with only faint apologies, devoting a brief paragraph to it. Calvin devoted much of Book III of the *Institutes,* on the means of grace, to prayer. Surely this is not an accurate way to prioritize. If so, I think the two traditions would part ways rather sharply here. The contemplative tradition obviously views prayer, defined as communion or communication with God, as the main means for getting in touch with the working of grace in our lives and thus for growing in grace. As I said earlier, prayer involves listening to God through Scriptures (and sermon), through experiences, through our communion with other believers and through sacraments. Would Calvin reject such a perspective?

At this point I would return to the reason for the close correspondences between these traditions. Insofar as I can see, they are due to something deliberate in the Reformed (especially the Puritan) tradition's efforts to reform the church more fully; namely, a return to the medieval contemplative mainstream to recover insight concerning sanctification. The Puritans differed from the medieval contemplatives chiefly in the ambitiousness of their plans. Where contemplatives tried to make saints of those in monasteries, the Puritans tried to make saints of everybody. Here the Puritans forgot one of their basic tenets—the fallenness of humanity—which precludes such optimism. The contemplatives were more realistic. Only those who really want to and are willing to surrender themselves fully can become saints. Coercion will never produce the kind of holy obedience God requires.

Sanctification is yielding our lives to God, then He will change us.

But we live in culture, church & Academia

The Wesleyan View

Laurence W. Wood

JOHN WESLEY FORMULATED NINETEEN EXACTING QUESTIONS TO BE asked of all Methodist ministers at the time of their ordination. The most jolting (some might say presumptuous) of these is the third question: "Do you expect to be made perfect in love in this life?"[1]

This expectation to be made perfect in love has differing interpretations in the Wesleyan tradition, and I would not be so presumptuous as to identify my perception as the only Wesleyan perspective. I do wish, however, to express what I believe is a truly viable Wesleyan interpretation.

In this regard, it should be kept in mind that a Wesleyan hermeneutic, though it gives priority to the Scriptures as the basis of all beliefs, assumes that all truth is existentially perceived and appropriated. One does not simply come to the Scriptures with a blank mind and then rationalistically interpret the Bible. For the Bible is always interpreted through experience, tradition and reason. This is not a subjectivizing of the biblical revelation, but a frank acknowledgement that all truth is mediated in a larger context, rather than merely through a logical and rationalistic framework. This personal-relational dimension is a decisive exegetical and theological presupposition for a Wesleyan hermeneutic. Hence the crucible of life is the laboratory for testing our interpretation of Scripture.

For Wesley, holiness is a process of becoming in reality what already is ours in Christ through the new birth. Holiness is the dialectic moment in which Christ's pure love *becomes* an inner reality for the believer. This dialectic moment is a *becoming*, a process. It is a continuous happening through the indwelling of the Spirit.

Though a scholar, Wesley's practical intent was to get right to the heart of what the gospel is all about and to make it available to the common person.[2] This center he identified as *Christian perfection*, as opposed to absolute perfection, Adamic perfection or angelic perfection. Christian perfection means "to be renewed in the image of Christ," which is simply to love God with all the heart, mind and soul. Wesley noted the many biblical passages which call the believer to this level of Christian experience. In so doing, he did not downplay the significance of the new birth. In fact, Wesley maintained that Paul taught that all justified believers are "sanctified," and thus he pointed out that one should make a distinction between sanctification and *entire sanctification* (a distinction he always assumed but rarely followed in practice).[3] Sanctification begins at the moment of the new birth; entire sanctification is the experience of being made perfect in love.

Wesley reminds us that this experience of being made perfect in love is not humanly possible to achieve except through faith as a gift of God's grace.[4] The argument often used against this possibility of grace in this life is that experience militates against it; hence it must be primarily an ideal! But where in Scripture are we led to believe it is an unrealizable ideal? The tenor of Scripture throughout is that we are expected to love God with all our hearts! Surely John's comments, for example, would suggest that some Christians are made perfect in love while others may not be (1 Jn 4:18).

Based on the testimony of Christian experience, as well as the Scriptures, Wesley maintained that the possibility of perfect love is realizable in this life. He assumed that if experience could not confirm his understanding of the doctrines of Scripture, he would then be persuaded that he had misread the Scriptures.[5] To be sure, for Wesley only the Scriptures could establish a doctrine, but experience was a necessary confirmation that he had properly understood the biblical texts. Hence his diaries are replete with the testimonies of persons who had professed to have received the gift of perfect love. So both Scriptures and experience led him to the conclusion that normally one receives the gift of perfect love subsequent to the new birth and often prior to death.[6]

A Second Blessing

Hence John Wesley used the phrases "a second blessing" and "a second rest," and he insisted that perfect love for God could be experienced "instantaneously."[7] However, holiness for Wesley was never a fetish of repeating ritualistic terms. It was not a static, intellectualized doctrine, nor a sinless perfection in which one would never fall short of sanctifying grace, but a life continuously lived and always in process.

This concept of a "second work of grace," however, should not be interpreted in a psychologically stifling manner, as if the number two were more important than the *life* to be lived. John Wesley counseled, in response to the question about when holiness should be experienced: "Ask that it may be done now; today, while it is called today. . . . Today is his time, as well as tomorrow. Make haste, man, make haste."[8] Unless one expects to love God with all one's heart, it is not likely that one will ever do it! That seems to me to be the intent of the logic of affirming entire sanctification as a *second* work of grace. Regardless of whether one comes to a perfect love for God gradually or instantaneously, the point is that one *expects* to be made perfect in love in this life. The *expectation* is the decisive thing! One expects it now and always! One receives it now, tomorrow and always!

Wesley was careful to point out that Christian perfection did not eliminate the human element. Although one could be freed from the power of sin, one is not freed from the consequences of sin in this life. One's heart could be perfectly devoted to Christ, but one's behavior was often defective. This means even those believers made perfect in love still need the atonement of Christ for their daily offenses. In a letter of April 7, 1763, he writes:

> The nicest point of all which relates to Christian perfection is that which you inquire of. Thus much is certain: they that love God with all their heart, and all men as themselves, are scripturally perfect. And surely such there are; otherwise the promise of God would be a mere mockery of human weakness. Hold fast this. But then re-

member, on the other hand, you have this treasure in an earthen vessel; you dwell in a poor, shattered house of clay, which presses down the immortal spirit. Hence all your thoughts, words, and actions are so imperfect; so far from coming up to the standard (that law of love, which, but for the corruptible body, your soul would answer in all instances), that you may well say till you go to him you love, "Every moment, Lord, I need the merit of Thy death."[9]

Christian perfection, furthermore, is to be distinguished from psychological perfectionism. It is helpful to remember that psychologically repressed complexes (and not necessarily a sinful heart) are often the sources of misconduct and imperfect behavior. Only God knows the heart, and it is inappropriate for us to pass judgment on other believers' experience because of their apparent misconduct. So long as we live in this fallen world, our behavior will never be perfect, even though the intentions of our hearts may be pure. To be sure, the gap between intention and performance should not be considerable. Paul confesses he knows nothing sinful in his own heart, but God finally will be his judge (1 Cor 4:4).

Of course, this observation must be carefully guarded from abuse by modern-day gnostics who would like to disavow responsibility for their actions. Whether acting intentionally or not, we are nonetheless responsible and accountable for our behavior. However, we are not the judge of the motives of other persons despite the defective nature of their behavior. This is the very point John Wesley made when he insisted that the doctrine of perfect love was not to be interpreted as sinless perfection. For all believers, even the most mature, daily fall short of the glory of God. In fact, the entirely sanctified are more aware of their weaknesses and sins and thus are more capable of growth in grace because of the openness of their hearts to their true situation. Their one desire is to be wholly committed to Jesus. With this loving and nonthreatening relationship to Christ, believers are enabled to be honest and open about themselves, and the Holy Spirit is able to provide valuable insights.

Christian perfection for Wesley then "never means a claim to flawlessness." It is precisely "the sanctifying and purgative action of the Holy Spirit" that enables the believer to be relieved and cleansed of these disordered contents of the unconscious mind.[10] In other words,

Christian perfection is a perfection of love which genuinely opens up the possibility for an honest and unpretentious relationship to Christ through his Spirit. This relationship enables us to grow in grace and to be inwardly healed of those negative and damaged emotions that continue to haunt and disrupt our human lives. It is an experience with Christ that is so embracing, so trusting and so accepting that one need not fear (1 Jn 4:18). There is no need for pretentious behavior and perfectionistic attitudes, for we knowingly and willingly recognize that our sufficiency is totally in the relationship with God through Christ. This level of relationship to Christ means that whatever hurts, whatever maladjustments, whatever sins that beset us, we are assured of Christ's forgiveness and cleansing through the power of his Holy Spirit. Genuine divine love (1 Cor 13) is accepting and forgiving, not condemning and berating. Assured of Christ's love, we are assured of our spiritual identity even though our psychological identity is only gradually formed in the context of the Christian community of love.

This concept of assurance is a distinctive emphasis of John Wesley. Whatever passing emotions they may feel threatened by, believers are possessed of an abiding conviction through the internal testimony of the Spirit that they are fully accepted of God in Christ. This acceptance means real "union with Christ" through the Spirit; this acceptance is not a mere "as if" we are righteous, but the believer really is righteous (1 Jn 4:12-13).

Entire Sanctification

Admittedly one of the possible psychological hang-ups may be associated with the term *entire* sanctification. That sounds like absolute perfection or angelic perfection—both of which Wesley distinguished from Christian perfection. Surely if one is *entirely* sanctified nothing possibly could be amiss in one's life.

However, it should be kept in mind that the word *entire* is not to be interpreted in a static, rationalistic manner. The word denotes a quality of being, not an abstract, quantitative measurement. Entire sanctification relates to the quality and purity of love (intent), not to the degree of love. It implies a pursuit of love, and only that. Why then should we use the word *entire* if it is so easily misunderstood and may have such terrible consequences psychologically? To be sure, one will want to use the phrase in a most judicious way. But we cannot simply solve semantical problems by avoiding the use of some words. After all, the word is thoroughly biblical. Paul says in 1 Thessalonians 5:23: "And the very God of peace sanctify you *entirely (holoteleis)*. And I pray God your entire *(holoklēron)* body and soul and spirit be preserved blameless" (but not faultless!). "Entire sanctification" is not a theological term first coined by John Wesley, but is used by Paul to describe the state of grace which he expected the Thessalonians to experience in order to be fully prepared for the coming of the Lord.

Two particular pieces of biblical imagery which Wesley used to describe the nature of perfect love are "Canaan Land" and "circumcision of heart." A third description was largely used by John Fletcher, who was also the first systematic theologian of Methodism. Fletcher's "favourite subject" (as Wesley put it in his biography of Fletcher)[11] was to describe the experience of perfect love in terms of being filled with the Spirit.

Concerning this latter description, Paul shows there is a historical distinction between the *sending of the Son* and the *sending of the Spirit*, and it can be implied that there is in the life of the believer an experiential distinction between receiving the Son and receiving the fullness of the Pentecostal Spirit (see Gal 4:4-7). Jesus' disciples, for example, were genuinely converted, as reported in Luke 10:20, before their subsequent experience with the Pentecostal Spirit. To be sure, the Spirit was with them before Pentecost, but he did not yet dwell in them (Jn 14:17). In their case their experience of the Son and the Spirit were historically distinct. It is also significant that Jesus said that only those who were already believers could receive the (fullness of the) Spirit (Jn 14:17). Yet there is a sense in which one could be "born of the Spirit" even before Pentecost (Jn 3:5), though after Pentecost one might receive the gift of the indwelling Spirit in his fullness (Jn 14:15-20; compare to Acts 2:4).

If one accepts at face value the accounts in Acts 8:14-17 and Acts 19:1-7, the Samaritans and the Ephesians illustrate the possibility that one may have faith in Christ and subsequently receive the fullness of the Pentecostal Spirit. Their personal Pentecost followed their personal experience of the resurrected life of Jesus. At least this perception has a longstanding existence both in the Catholic and the Wesleyan traditions.[12] To assume that the Pentecostal accounts in Acts are only re-flecting a missionary situation unique to the primitive church is an inadequate view of salvation history.

While there is this unique reception of the Spirit in the life of the believer subsequent to the new birth, it is the same Spirit whom we receive at conversion. Devotionally speaking, there is no difference between Christ and the Holy Spirit, for the Spirit is the exalted Christ, as Paul tells us in 2 Corinthians 3:18. Strictly and theologically speaking, there is a real difference among the Father, Son and Holy Spirit, but it is a difference-in-unity. This triunity of God's being means that whatever unique function one of the divine persons has, the other divine persons also share in the same activity. The concept of the Trinity does not mean that there are three independent centers of consciousness within the divine life. Nor do the progressive stages of Christian experience lend themselves to the notion that one can have the Son without the Spirit, as if the Christian life were made up of disjointed events. We can certainly speak of the deeper Christian life as the fullness of the Spirit without minimizing the reception of Christ in conversion, even as we can speak of the unique coming of the Spirit on the day of Pentecost as a deeper revelation of God without minimizing the person of Jesus Christ in his earthly ministry. The Spirit of Pentecost is the continuation of the earthly Jesus. Even as there were stages in salvation in which God was progressively known as Father, Son and Holy Spirit, so there may be stages in one's personal history of salvation in which one may know God successively as Father, Son and Holy Spirit. Yet it is the one and same God who is known. The dispensation of the Spirit signifies that the fullness of the triune God has been revealed and that this fullness is given to the believer in Christ.

A weakness of some exegetes who wish to interpret Acts as merely history, while referring to the epistles as the more adequate basis for formulating theology, fail to see that biblical history is primarily theological and existential in its essence. Those who, for example, restrict the time distinction between the reception of Christ and the infilling of the Spirit as a mere historical sequence limited to the book of Acts may be assuming a static and rationalistic view of history. They fail to see that the once-and-for-all events of the past, as Easter and Pentecost, are to become contemporary events in our own personalized history of salvation. It is not adequate to interpret the book of Acts as if it intended simply to be a positivistic record of redemptive events—as if the pattern of events reflected in the lives of the disciples, the Samaritans and the Ephesians had no bearing on the pattern of events in our personal lives today. To be sure, Pentecost marks the decisive beginning of the church as the vestibule into the kingdom of God, but Pentecost also marks in a decisive manner our own personal completion in Christ as we appropriate that event for ourselves.

John Fletcher provided a clear exposition of the meaning of Christian experience in terms of a trinitarian dispensationalism (not to be confused with Scofield's dispensationalism). He interpreted Christian experience in progressive stages corresponding to God's revelation as Father, Son and Holy Spirit. Some have faith in God as Father who is Creator; some have faith in God as Son who is Redeemer; others have faith in the Holy Spirit who is Sanctifier. Fletcher believes the Apostles' Creed implies these three stages of faith.[13]

Fletcher's distinction among the dispensations is similar to the thought of Wesley, who also points out "that there are several stages in Christian life, as in natural [life]." Some people are like mere babes, others are like young adults. The highest stage of the Christian life is likened to that of parents, who know "the Father, and the Son, and the Spirit of Christ, in [their] inmost soul. [They] are 'perfect men,' being grown up to 'the measure of the stature of the fullness of Christ.' "[14]

In *A Plain Account of Christian Perfection,* Wesley equates perfect love with being "full of His Spirit."[15] Wesley also speaks of the possibility of Christian perfection because there has "been a larger measure of the Holy Spirit given under the Gospel than under the Jewish dispensation."[16] In a letter to Joseph Benson, Wesley equates perfect love with being filled with the Spirit.[17] Wesley further equates "the fruit of the Spirit" in its entirety with Christian perfection. It is the "fruit of the Spirit" that is the witness of the children of God "in the highest sense" (in other words, those entirely sanctified) in contrast to the children of God "in the lowest sense" (in other words, the justified believer).[18]

Exodus and Conquest

It seems to me that a dispensational exposition of Christian experience is truly biblical. Certainly it had been largely appropriated by the nineteenth-century holiness tradition with varying shifts of emphasis and adaptation to the American revivalistic movement, as Melvin Dieter has shown.[19]

The key for seeing this truth lies in our understanding of the narrative view of history that the Bible assumes. In the Bible, history is not a mere record of the past; history is the dynamic synthesis of the past, the present and the future. What happened once-and-for-all in the past is still an available experience for today; what will happen in the future is also available in a measure for us today.

This continuity of history is essential for an understanding of the typological relationship between the Old and New Testaments. In particular, the book of Acts assumes a typological continuity with the history of the Old Testament. For example, the theological simplicity of the sermons in Acts 1—13 is in keeping with the simplicity which is characteristic of Israel's earliest cultic confessions, which are a simple recital of God's mighty historical acts in behalf of his people. Significantly, these apostolic sermons in Acts assume a close connection between the events of Jesus' life and the exodus-conquest themes of the Old Testament.

Typical of Israel's earliest cultic confessions is Deuteronomy 26:5-15. These confessions recall the history of the exodus and the conquest from the past as events for the present worshipers to experience for themselves. Of special significance in these cultic confessions is the narrative use of the plural pronoun "we" which suggests the involvement of the worshiper in the two decisive saving acts of Yahweh—the exodus and the conquest. These two events are as salvific for the present experience of the worshiper as they were for the contemporaries of Moses and Joshua. Likewise, the resurrection of Jesus from the dead and the Pentecostal gift of his Spirit are salvific, not only because they happened at a dateable period of time in the history of the world, but because each person experiences (re-enacts) for him or herself Jesus' resurrected life and the indwelling of his Spirit.

The book of Acts thus reflects in the closest possible manner the connection between the history of Jesus and the history of Israel. This relationship is so closely linked that the apostles see nothing in their kerygma which is not already implicit in the ancient credo. Their worship, their ritual and their preaching assume a direct relationship to the history of Israel. The essence of that relationship is that the promise to Abraham had its fulfillment in Jesus. To be sure, Abraham comes before Jesus Christ in chronological time, but Jesus in a sense comes before Abraham (Jn 8:58). While the history of Jesus is a continuation of the history of Israel, there is a sense in which it can be said that the salvation history of Israel is dependent on the "future" history of Jesus. This flexibility and qualified reversibility of history and time is an assumption of the biblical history of salvation.

A fundamental implication of the relationship between Israel and Jesus is that the historical pattern of God's dealing with ancient Israel is embraced in the history of Jesus. It is this concept of a historical pattern linking the history of Israel and the history of Jesus that brings us to the very center of the apostolic preaching. The substance of this historical pattern can be stated in this thematic way: Jesus' resurrection from the dead and Pentecost are events theologically parallel to Israel's exodus from Egyptian captivity and the possession of the Promised Land. In this respect, the exodus and conquest events prefigure the resurrection and Pentecostal events.

It should be remembered that the whole intent of God's promise to Abraham in bringing his people to Canaan was that there they could have a place to worship God and to love him perfectly (Deut 6:1-5). Failure to love God perfectly meant exile, and their subsequent return to Canaan would be possible because at that time their hearts would be circumcised, enabling them to love God perfectly (Deut 30:6). This hope for a return to Canaan was the theme of the prophets as they foresaw the Spirit outpoured upon the people whose hearts would then be cleansed by the Spirit (Ezek 37:14, 27-28).

Pentecost was the initial fulfillment of this eschatological expectation. The Spirit of the exalted Christ had now come to take up his abode, not in the physical land of Canaan which was a type (Exodus 15:17), but in the hearts of believers. Now the kingdom had "already" come and the righteousness of God was truly accessible to all because their hearts could be cleansed and empowered to love God perfectly. Canaan as a type of the kingdom is realized in the Pentecostal inauguration of the church. The Abrahamic blessing and promise is thus actualized at Pentecost, though there remains a "not yet" aspect of the coming kingdom.

Alan Richardson shows that "there can be no doubt that it was upon the historical experiences of the *deliverance from Egypt* and the *establishment in Canaan* that the fundamental certainty of all biblical faith was based" (emphasis mine).[20] He further points out: "But it is uniquely the genius of the Bible that the historical is transmuted by the eschatological, so that the action of God in the past becomes the type or foreshadowing of his action in the future."[21] Richardson then shows that these saving events are not just events of the past. Rather, "the salvation that was once-for-all wrought for the whole people is appropriated by each family or each individual as the family or the individual makes response in worship and thanksgiving (Ex 12:26-27; Deut 6:20-25; 26:1-11; Jn 6:53-58; 1 Cor 10:16-17; 11:23-26)."[22] In reference to the exodus event in particular, Richardson writes:

> The act of deliverance, so to speak, remains active and potent throughout the continuing history of the people for whom it was wrought; in the biblical view it is not a mere event of the past, but something that is ever and again made present and real in the lives of those who celebrate it in word and sacrament.[23]

These two themes—the exodus and the conquest—became for all subsequent time in the history of Israel the normative pattern of God's dealing with his people. For example, the liturgy of Israel extolling the salvation of God (compare Ps 68; 77:11-20; 78; 114; 136:10-22) focuses on these two decisive events. The *credo* of Deuteronomy 26:5-15 is a reliving and personalizing of these two saving events. During their exile and captivity, the prophets envisaged Israel's salvation through a new exodus and a new conquest which would restore the Davidic kingdom in the Promised Land.

In this respect, Edmond Jacob also shows that the exodus and conquest events were not merely the *formative* events of Israel's national beginnings, but rather they were the events on which every Israelite experienced his or her own redemption. What happened to the nation of Israel as a whole was to be appropriated personally by every individual Israelite in all generations. Jacob writes:

> At the Passover feast, the departure from Egypt was enacted through the ritual, so clearly that it may be said that at least once a year the exodus ceased to be a fact of the past and became a living reality, and that never, even after five centuries, did the Israelites

er themselves different from their ancestors who, under
? guidance, had experienced the deliverance (see Amos 3:2).
. . . The *credo* of Deuteronomy 26 mentions the entry into Canaan
as a second article; the deliverance of the exodus was only made with
a view to the possession of the country.[24]

Thus we see that the exodus and conquest were both the *formative* and
normative events that formed a pattern for the salvation of every Israelite in every new generation. The Passover feast was no mere memorial;
rather, it was a personal appropriation of the exodus event in the
present.

This exodus-conquest pattern in achieving the Abrahamic promise
is also decisive for the history of Jesus. In this respect, G. E. Wright
says these two events "are as important for the New Testament as for
the Old. In Christ is the new exodus and the new inheritance."[25] The
earliest apostolic kerygma presupposes this theme. The exodus becomes a type of the resurrection in the New Testament, and the conquest is a type of Pentecost.

The Bible makes extensive use of types, as von Rad has shown.[26] A
type is different from an allegory. In typology, history and literal meaning are taken seriously, but in allegory history and literal meaning are
largely irrelevant. One of the reasons why types are an important factor
in the Bible is because of the feeling that believers participate in the
whole sweep of history. This existential feeling of participation means
that we are as involved in the past and the future as we are in the present
moment. God is the Lord of history, and his actions in the past are
types of what he will do in the future.

The Lord brought Israel out of Egyptian bondage through the exodus event and brought them into the Promised Land of Canaan
through the conquest of the impure and ungodly Canaanites. This
Lord became incarnate in Jesus of Nazareth and was resurrected from
the dead, liberating us from the bondage of sin. He then sent his Holy
Spirit at Pentecost to indwell us as his temple so that we would have
power to conquer all that is impure and ungodly, so that we may have
clean hearts and a pure love for him alone. This same God desires for
us to have our own personal Easter and Pentecost now, in this moment,
for this moment can be a representation of the once-for-all event of the
past salvific events.

Pentecost marks the historical inauguration of the coming kingdom of righteousness with an ongoing personalized existential meaning. The Pentecostal reception of the Spirit denotes the confirming, establishing, sanctifying grace of God begun at conversion. Hence there are two initiatory steps into the kingdom—Easter and Pentecost. However, it should be stressed that these two stages are not absolutely distinct as if they were only extrinsically related. Though they are distinct in time, they are also related through time. Rather than a break existing between them, they exist in a continuum. Hence sanctifying grace (Pentecost theme) is really begun in justification (resurrection theme).

In *Pentecostal Grace* I have shown that the language of exodus is used in the New Testament to describe Jesus' resurrection from the dead. I have also shown that the language of Canaan is the language of Pentecost. The Easter event accentuates forgiveness of sins; the Pentecostal event accentuates the righteousness of the kingdom. I have also shown that these two events are the sole bases of the Christian life—an exegetical conclusion supported in tradition and in recent scholarship as in the writings of Karl Barth.[27]

One illustration of Canaan language as descriptive of Pentecost is the word *lot* (*klēros*), which recalls the apportioning of the tribes in the land of Canaan. In Acts 8:21, Peter says to Simon Magus: "You have neither *part* nor *lot* in this matter" (RSV; emphasis mine). Arndt and Gingrich point out the parallel between Acts 8:21 and Deuteronomy 12:12.[28] Cremer has shown that *part* (*meros*) and *lot* (*klēros*) are used together as a technical designation of Israel's possession of Canaan Land (Deut 10:9; 12:12; 14:27, 29; 18:1; Is 57:6).[29] It is highly significant that these words are used in this context, since undoubtedly Peter was presupposing that the kingdom established in Canaan Land prefigured the kingdom of Christ which was established on earth through the gift of the Holy Spirit.

Simon Magus had attempted to obtain the gift of God, that is, the Pentecostal gift of the Spirit, with money (Acts 8:18-19). Peter informed him that he was not prepared to receive this gift, for repentance (resurrection theme) is the prerequisite for receiving this gift (Pentecost theme, vv. 22-23). It is also significant that as a result of Philip's preaching the Samaritans had been converted through "receiving the Word of God" and being baptized (resurrection theme). Three days later Peter came to Samaria so that they might receive the Spirit (Pentecost theme) through the laying on of hands. With the exception of Simon Magus, the Samaritans were prepared to receive the Pentecostal Spirit, since they had already experienced their exodus from sin's captivity by believing and receiving the word of God (8:12, 14). On the other hand, Simon Magus did not have a proper relationship to Christ which was the prerequisite for receiving the Spirit: "You have neither part nor lot in this matter, for your heart is not right before God. Repent therefore of this wickedness of yours, and pray to the Lord that, if possible, the intent of your heart may be forgiven you" (Acts 8:21-22 RSV).

Peter is saying to Simon Magus that since he has not experienced an exodus from spiritual captivity, he is not prepared to receive the inheritance. After all, the inheritance is promised only to those who have made their exodus from captivity. That is, there can be no conquest until first there has been an exodus. This means there can be no Pentecost for him until he has experienced Jesus' resurrected life which is signified in Christian baptism. He has "neither part nor lot in this matter" of entering into the promised rest, because he is still living in the captivity of wickedness and unrepentance.

Often the language of Canaan Land has been reserved as a description for heaven, an element which is implicit in this language. Heaven is the final abode of God's saints where they will worship him perfectly after their glorification. But a more complete understanding of the language of Canaan Land links it to the concept of the kingdom of God. To be sure, this kingdom will be consummated for us in heaven, but recent biblical scholarship has pointed out that the dominant idea of the kingdom in the New Testament is that the kingdom of God is "already" come, though it is "not yet" come. The "already" aspect is the thrust of the New Testament as C. H. Dodd has already pointed out—though he too easily obscured its futuristic aspect.[30] That the kingdom had already come is reflected in the New Testament appropriation of Canaan Land language to describe the nature of present Christian experience suggested in such terms as riches, fruit, joy, sanctification, rest, abiding, dwelling, inheritance and peace.

One phrase in particular which Wesley used to describe the nature of Christian perfection is the "rest of faith." In this respect, he equates "the rest which remaineth for the people of God" (Heb 4:9) as descriptive of Christian perfection. John Calvin also identified Canaan Land as a symbol of sanctification by faith. Yet this "spiritual rest" which cleanses one of "inbred corruption" (as Calvin puts it) is not fully realized in this life, though the believer is "striving" for it only in the sense of approximating an ideal.[31] For Wesley, the "striving" is to be realized "today" (Heb 4:7). Today by faith one can have this spiritual rest and a pure love for God.

> Lord, I believe a rest remains
>   To all Thy people known;
> A rest where pure enjoyment reigns,
>   And Thou art loved alone.
>
> A rest where all our soul's desire
>   Is fixed on things above;
> Where doubt, and pain, and fear expire,
>   Cast out by perfect love.
>
> Come, Father, Son, and Holy Ghost,
>   And seal me Thine abode!
> Let all I am in Thee be lost;
>   Let all be lost in God.[32]

Circumcision of the Heart

Wesley also used the covenantal language of circumcision as descriptive of Christian perfection. Wesley defined circumcision of the heart as "that habitual disposition of soul which, in the sacred writings, is termed holiness; and which directly implies, the being cleansed from sin, 'from all filthiness both of flesh and spirit'; and, by consequence, the being endued with those virtues which were also in Christ Jesus; the being so 'renewed in the spirit of our mind,' as to be 'perfect as our Father in heaven is perfect.' "[33] In May 1765 he wrote to a friend: "January 1, 1733, I preached the sermon on the Circumcision of the Heart, which contains all that I now teach concerning salvation from all sin, and loving God with an undivided heart. . . . This was then, as it is now, my idea of perfection."[34]

The rite of circumcision implied the idea of cleansing. More specifically, the (inherited) flesh excised in the formal rite of circumcision prefigured the New Testament concept of being cleansed from original (inherited) sin "by putting off the body of flesh in the circumcision of Christ" (Col 2:11 RSV). Walther Eichrodt shows that circumcision and cleansing form a single theme and that the rite of circumcision was altogether replaced with its spiritual meaning of cleansing in the prophets.[35]

That circumcision was understood as signifying cleanness must be understood first and foremost in the light of Israel's absolutely unique concept of God's holiness and transcendence as opposed to human sinfulness. Circumcision was "a symbol of the purification and sanctification of the whole life" because it symbolized living in the presence of God.[36]

It is significant that Paul links the concept of the flesh *(sarx)* with the idea of original sin, or inherited sin (Col 2:13). The sin of Adam which has been passed on to every person (Rom 5:12-19) is labeled the "flesh" (Rom 7:14). As S. J. De Vries shows, Paul identifies "the flesh" with "the principle of sin which lies within the heart" and is thus "responsible for the unruliness of these desires" (Rom 13:14; Gal 5:16-21).[37]

Rudolf Bultmann's exposition is especially illuminating for seeing the relationship between the rite of circumcision and Paul's use of the word *sarx*. Bultmann shows that for Paul the original sin of Adam (Rom 5:12-19) is an attitude of pride and self-sufficiency. This Pauline concept of the flesh is in no way associated with Greek dualistic thought, as if he were implying that the physical flesh is sinful while the immaterial spirit is holy. Rather, when Paul speaks of the flesh as sinful it is a metaphor derived from the Old Testament practice of the circumcision of the flesh which had already been spiritualized into an ethical meaning.[38]

Gerhard von Rad has shown that the circumcision of heart in Deuteronomy 30:6 and Jeremiah 4:4 is directly connected with the idea of cleanness in Jeremiah 31:31-34, 32:29-41 and Ezekial 36:24-36.[39] The formal rite of circumcision, like the sacrificial rites in general, was of no interest to the prophets, but they nonetheless stressed its spiritual implication for cleanness of heart which was to be achieved through the outpouring of the Spirit under the New Covenant.

This prophetic concept of the outpouring of the Spirit as effecting the cleansing of the heart is the meaning of Pentecostal grace. This can be seen both in Acts 15:8-9 and Romans 2:28-29 where the cleansing (circumcision) of the heart is the result of the gift of the Holy Spirit. In this respect, sanctification is identified primarily with the work of the Holy Spirit (1 Pet 1:2).

The Pauline concept of sinful flesh is the very opposite of the Spirit-filled life (Rom 8:9). The flesh is all that is contrary to the will of God (Gal 5:19). The flesh is the course of sinful deeds. Hence Paul differentiates between the flesh as a spiritual defect in one's character, on the one hand, and sinful deeds as the manifestation of that spiritual defect, on the other hand (see Gal 5:17, 19, 24). In Colossians 2:13, Paul speaks of this twofold nature of sin as "dead in trespasses" (sinful actions) and "the uncircumcision of your flesh" (original sin as the source of sinful actions). This twofold distinction between "sins" (actions) and "the sin" (the inherited condition which is the source of sins) is the theological basis for a distinction between justification (forgiveness of sins) and sanctification (cleansing from the condition of sin and an empowering with perfect love for God).

Bultmann shows that for Paul inherited sin is not something for which he is responsible per se, but "by his concrete 'transgression' " he becomes "jointly responsible" with Adam for his sin.[40] John Fletcher, in reference to Romans 5:18, also writes: "We are *no way* accountable for our moral infection, yet it cannot be denied that we are answerable for our obstinate refusal of relief, and for the *willful neglect* of the means found out by Divine mercy for our cure."[41] This distinction between original sin (for which we are not directly responsible) and actual sins (for which we are directly responsible) is an important distinction for Wesley's and Fletcher's concept of salvation. In justification one is liberated from the dominion of sin, one's sins are forgiven, and sanctification is begun. In entire sanctification, one experiences the gift of perfect love and the sinful being, figuratively speaking, is cleansed.

Bultmann argues persuasively that the Pauline emphasis is thus not on justification ("forgiveness of sins") but rather on sanctification ("freedom from sin"). Paul focuses his attack on the source of sins—

the inherited sinful flesh.[42]

Krister Stendahl has termed Paul's sense of his freedom from the power of sin "a robust consciousness." He has shown that Paul felt himself to be a person whom Christ had truly made holy and free from sin. Paul's attitude about himself shows little indication of a troubled conscience. Stendahl also shows that Luther's struggle with conscience has been wrongly interpreted as typical of Paul. Stendahl's exposition of the following passages substantiates this emphasis that Paul felt himself to have been made a truly good and holy person through Jesus Christ: Acts 23:1; 24:16; 1 Cor 9:27; Rom 9:1; 2 Cor 1:12; 2 Cor 5:10f.; 1 Cor 4:4; 2 Cor 12:9-10. Stendahl writes:

> The famous formula "simul justus et peccator"—at the same time righteousness and sinner—as a description of the status of the Christian may have some foundation in the Pauline writings, but this formula cannot be substantiated as the center of Paul's conscious attitude toward his personal sins. Apparently, Paul did not have a type of introspective conscience which such a formula seems to presuppose. This is probably one of the reasons why "forgiveness of sins" is the term of salvation which is used least of all in the Pauline writings.[43]

This emphasis on the actual possibility of freedom from sin is intelligible only if the distinction between the ethical and the legal ideas of sin is kept in mind. Wesley speaks of this distinction in terms of voluntary (ethical) and involuntary (legal) transgressions. He interprets the concept of sinning in Scripture to denote voluntary transgressions of the known will of God. However, Wesley also allowed for the validity of a legal definition of sin which meant that involuntary transgressions are also serious and need the atonement of Christ. Wesley writes: "The most perfect have continual need of the merits of Christ, even for their actual transgressions, and may say, for themselves, as well as for their brethren, 'Forgive us our trespasses.' " Hence Wesley says that "many mistakes [involuntary transgressions] may coexist with pure love."[44]

That the ethical definition of sin is the normal meaning of sin in Scripture can easily be tested. For example, Wesley shows that the idea that sin is the transgression of the will of God (1 Jn 3:4) is not the same as saying that every transgression is a sin. Otherwise John's assertion that everyone who sins is of the devil becomes unintelligible (1 Jn 3:8). If 1 John 3:8 is interpreted to mean: "Everyone who voluntarily and involuntarily transgresses the will of God is of the devil," then everyone presumably must be condemned, since it is apparent that no one can claim that his or her actions are perfect. It does not lessen the force of this conclusion to argue that John was only speaking of those who *habitually* transgress, since everyone does in fact habitually and involuntarily transgress the will of God. Only if the biblical demand to cease from sinning is interpreted ethically (to refrain from voluntary transgressions) can it be made intelligible. This ethical meaning of sin can be likewise tested in reference to most uses of sin in the New Testament.

This distinction between the ethical and legal definitions of sin is implicit in the Levitical sacrificial system. If one committed an involuntary sin and it became known, he or she was to offer immediately a sacrifice as an atonement (see Lev 4:13-15). Yet once a year on the Day of Atonement the high priest offered up a sacrifice to atone for involuntary sins of ignorance (Lev 16; compare to Heb 9:7).

Sins, whether voluntary or involuntary, are our responsibility and we are accountable to God for them; hence they need to be atoned for. But voluntary sins carry a special degree of ethical seriousness about them because of one's willful involvement in what is contrary to God's will. Circumcision of heart better enables one to live a victorious life over sinning because one is cleansed from sin. Even so, one's life is characterized by transgressions which may be motivated by psychologically repressed complexes or involuntary influences. The heart may be blameless, but one's performance imperfect. That one can have perfect intent with imperfect behavior is illustrated by the Levitical law which distinguished between those transgressions which are committed "wittingly" and those which are committed "unwittingly." Only if the ethical-relational dimensions of being cleansed from all sin are assumed can the concept of Christian perfection be intelligible. To think of sin as an entity that is literally extracted like a decayed tooth implies a number of confusions, not the least of which is a materialistic view of reality. An ethical interpretation of the cleansing of the heart from all sin in the contemporary language of psychology has a relational and interpersonal meaning; it implies having an appropriate self-orientation through a wholehearted regard for God and others.

This level of ethical living above sin was implied in the initial insti-
tution of the rite of circumcision. In Genesis 17:1, God commands
Abraham to "walk before me, and be thou perfect" (KJV). The word
perfect (*tāmîn*) does not mean faultless. Von Rad shows that it denotes
perfect intent of the heart. It implies a perfect relationship to God. "It
signifies complete, unqualified surrender." Hence circumcision has a
"typological correspondence" (von Rad's term) to perfection of heart.
As von Rad puts it, this perfection symbolized in Abraham's circumcision means "it is the constraint of his whole life which is henceforth
to be lived in the presence of this revealed God (life is a 'walk,' a
'walking about')."[45]

This circumcision which enables one to walk blamelessly before the
Lord is accomplished through the fullness of the Spirit (Rom 2:28-29).
This is seen in Acts 15:8-9. "And God who knows the heart bore
witness to them, giving them the Holy Spirit just as he did to us [at
Pentecost]; and he made no distinction between us and them, but
cleansed their hearts by faith" (RSV). The inherited flesh was excised
by the infilling of the Spirit, figuratively speaking.

John Fletcher specifically relates this cleansing in Acts 15:9 to Wesley's concept of Christian perfection. He points out that Cornelius, as
well as the disciples on the day of Pentecost, experienced cleansing
from all sin (spiritual circumcision) through the fullness of the Holy
Spirit.[46] That Cornelius's *cleansing* implied total deliverance from original sin is seen through its equation with the idea of circumcision (Acts
10:1—11:18; 15:1-11). Even as circumcision symbolized sanctification
through the excision of the physical flesh, so the cleansing of the Holy
Spirit meant for Cornelius the purification of his heart from the sinful
flesh.

Consequently, it is not without biblical warrant that Wesley speaks
of entire sanctification as the cleansing of the heart from "all inbred
sin" and being "saved from all sin." He further describes original sin
figuratively as "leprosy," "the evil root," "the carnal mind."[47] The essence of original sin is carnal pride; the essence of Christian perfection
is pure love for God. Wesley says it is pointless to debate whether
freedom from "original sin" means it is "suspended, or extinguished."
Rather, he says that "it is enough that they feel nothing but love."[48] In

other words, sin is not literally a "thing," but it is an attitude of pride that alienates one from God and others. Sanctification is love for God and others. Sanctification has thus to do with *intent*. In a letter to his sister, Wesley thus points out the danger of overstating the claims of what perfection of love means. He says "perfection is consistent with a thousand nervous disorders." Wesley says "to overdo" the claims of perfection is "to undo" it. For then it will be unbelievable.[49]

Another parallel covenantal concept to spiritual circumcision is the Pauline concept of being "*sealed* with the promised Holy Spirit" (Eph 1:13 RSV). An exposition of circumcision as a seal will indicate this relationship.

Circumcision was the seal of the covenant with Abraham that his posterity would become a nation and that they would occupy Canaan Land (Gen 12:2, 7). In this respect, circumcision as a seal pointed to the fact that a holy God, a holy people and a holy land would form "an indissoluble triad."[50]

A seal is a confirmation; it is an imprint of the reality; it is the reality realized in a provisional way. Circumcision as a seal was thus the pre-actualization of the promise of Canaan Land which God had made to Abraham some fourteen years earlier when Abraham had first believed God. In a qualified sense, Abraham's circumcision was his conquest event which came subsequent to his justifying experience. It was the proleptic event of the crossing of the Jordan River into Canaan Land.

In the light of this linking of circumcision and the Promised Land, it becomes highly significant that upon the Israelites' immediate crossing of the Jordan River into Canaan, circumcision was performed on all uncircumcised males. The crossing into Canaan Land accompanied by the rite of circumcision meant "the reproach of Egypt" was removed (Josh 5:9). Not only had they been taken out of Egypt, but Egypt had now at last been taken out of them. Circumcision was the symbolic appropriation of the possession of the Promised Land; it specifically denoted actualized righteousness and perfect love.

The circumcision of Abraham denoted, in a figurative way, the sanctifying grace under the Pentecostal era of the New Covenant. To be sealed with the Pentecostal Spirit is to be stamped with the righteousness of Christ. It is to experience the actuality and righteousness of Christ. Wesley interprets Ephesians 4:30 this way:

The being "sealed by the Spirit" in the full sense of the word I take to imply two things: first, the receiving of the whole image of God, the whole mind which was in Christ, as the wax receives the whole impression of the seal when it is strongly and properly applied; secondly, the full assurance of hope, or a clear and permanent confidence of being with God in glory.[51]

In Ephesians 5:18-19, Paul shows that being "filled with the Holy Spirit" enables one to love God with all the heart: "Be filled with the Spirit, addressing one another in psalms and hymns and spiritual songs, singing and making melody to the Lord with all your heart"— in other words, worshiping and loving the Lord with *all the heart.* This is the essence of being filled with the Spirit—wholehearted devotion to God. Being filled with the Spirit is the essence of perfect love.

The concept of being Spirit-filled corresponds to the Pauline definition of a "real Jew" whose circumcision is of the Spirit (Rom 2:29). Circumcision signified entire devotion to God (Gen 17:1) and perfect love (Deut 30:6), and under the New Covenant of Pentecostal grace, heart-circumcision became a living reality through the outpouring of the Holy Spirit. Heart-circumcision, perfect love and being filled with the Spirit are conceptually identical in Pauline thought.

E. Stanley Jones's writings on holiness represent the best in devotional literature. His devotional thoughts on the Spirit-filled life serve as a worthy supplement to Wesley's sermons and hymns. He is a modern-day apostle of the sanctified life in practical terms. His writings challenge the church to move beyond "the pre-Pentecostal stage" to a Spirit-filled life, from a "with" to a "within" experience of the Spirit. One of his devotional prayers breathes the spirit of Wesley's view of sanctification:

O Spirit of God, I, too, long for this withinness—I would be every whit whole. I would have the seat of Thy authority within me. For I cannot conceive that Thou hast come so far in Thy redemption and wilt not come the full way. Thou wilt not stop on the threshold— Thou wilt move within. Come, Spirit, come—within, within, entirely within. Amen.[51]

Notes

[1]*The Book of Discipline of the United Methodist Church* (Nashville: The United Methodist

Publishing House, 1976), p. 422.

[2]John Wesley, "Preface to the Sermons," *The Standard Sermons of John Wesley,* ed. E. H. Sugden (London: Epworth Press, 1921), 1:30.

[3]Harald Lindstrom, *Wesley and Sanctification* (Nashville: Abingdon, 1946), p. 127.

[4]John Wesley, "The Character of a Methodist," *The Works of John Wesley,* ed. Thomas Jackson (London: Epworth Press, 1831), 8:341ff.; Wesley, "The Scripture Way of Salvation," *Standard Sermons* 2:453, 456-57.

[5]Wesley, *Works,* 5:129, 133.

[6]John Wesley, *A Plain Account of Christian Perfection* (London: Epworth Press, 1952), pp. 33, 36, 58, 112.

[7]Wesley, "Repentance of Believers," *Standard Sermons,* 2:391; Wesley, *A Plain Account,* pp. 41, 112.

[8]Wesley, *A Plain Account,* p. 54.

[9]Wesley, *Works,* 13:278-79.

[10]John Wesley, *Clinical Theology* (London: Darton Longman and Todd, 1966), p. xxv.

[11]Wesley, *Works,* 11:306.

[12]Laurence Wood, *Pentecostal Grace* (Grand Rapids, Mich.: Zondervan, 1982), pp. 240-57.

[13]John Fletcher, *Checks to Antinomianism* (New York: Hunt and Eaton, 1889), 1:590-91.

[14]Wesley, *Standard Sermons,* 2:157.

[15]Wesley, *A Plain Account,* p. 55.

[16]Ibid., p. 61.

[17]John Wesley, *The Letters of John Wesley,* ed. John Telford (London: Epworth Press, 1921), 5:229.

[18]Wesley, *A Plain Account,* pp. 78-79.

[19]Melvin Dieter, *Holiness Revival of the Nineteenth Century* (Metuchen, N. J.: Scarecrow Press, 1980). My book *Pentecostal Grace* intends to provide a biblical and theological basis for this understanding, while at the same avoiding some of the excesses the holiness tradition has at times engaged in.

[20]Alan Richardson, "Salvation, Savior," *The Interpreter's Dictionary of the Bible,* ed. George A. Buttrick (Nashville: Abingdon, 1962), 4:170.

[21]Ibid.

[22]Ibid., 4:172.

[23]Ibid.

[24]Edmond Jacob, *Theology of the Old Testament,* trans. Arthur W. Heathcote and Philip J. Allcock (New York: Harper, 1958), p. 191.

[25]George Ernest Wright, *God Who Acts* (Naperville, Ill.: A. R. Allenson, 1958), p. 63.

[26]Gerhard von Rad, *Old Testament Theology,* trans. D. M. G. Stalker (New York: Harper and Row, 1965), 2:365ff.

[27]Karl Barth, *Church Dogmatics,* trans. and ed. G. W. Bromiley (New York: Harper & Row, 1962), 4:4:30-52; see F. H. Durrwell, *The Resurrection,* trans. Rosemary Sheed (New York: Sheed and Ward, 1961), p. 315.

[28]Walter Bauer et al., ed., trans. William F. Arndt, *A Greek-English Lexicon of the New Testament* (Chicago: University of Chicago Press, 1957), p. 506.

[29]Hermann Cremer, *Biblico-Theological Lexicon of New Testament Greek,* trans. William Urwick, 4th ed., rev. (Edinburgh: T. & T. Clark, 1962), 1:357.

[30]C. H. Dodd, *The Parables of the Kingdom* (New York: Scribners, 1961), p. 35.

[31]John Calvin, *Commentaries on the Epistle of Paul the Apostle to the Hebrews,* trans. John

Owen (Grand Rapids, Mich.: Eerdmans, 1948), pp. 98-99.

[32]Wesley, *A Plain Account,* pp. 26-27.

[33]Wesley, *Standard Sermons,* 1:267-68.

[34]Ibid., 1:265.

[35]Walther Eichrodt, *Theology of the Old Testament,* trans. J. A. Baker (Philadelphia: Westminster, 1961), 1:138-39.

[36]Gustov Friedrich Oehler, *Theology of the Old Testament,* trans. George E. Day (New York: Funk and Wagnalls, 1883), p. 194.

[37]Alan Richardson, "Sin, Sinners," *Interpreter's Dictionary,* 4:373.

[38]Rudolf Bultmann, *Theology of the New Testament,* trans. Kendrick Grobel, 2 vols. (New York: Charles Scribner's Sons, 1951), 1:234-35, 241, 245, 253.

[39]Gerhard von Rad, *Deuteronomy, A Commentary,* trans. Dorothea Barton (Philadelphia: Westminster, 1966), pp. 183-84.

[40]Bultmann, *Theology of the New Testament,* 1:253.

[41]*The Works of the Reverend John Fletcher,* ed. John Gilpin (Salem, Oh.: Schmul Publishing, 1974), 3:320-21.

[42]Bultmann, *Theology of the New Testament,* 1:287.

[43]Krister Stendahl, *Paul among Jews and Gentiles* (Philadelphia: Fortress, 1976), pp. 82ff.

[44]Wesley, *A Plain Account,* pp. 42-43, 45-46.

[45]Gerhard von Rad, *Genesis, A Commentary,* trans. John H. Marks (Philadelphia: Westminster, 1972), p. 198.

[46]Fletcher, *Checks to Antinomianism,* 2:645.

[47]Wesley, *Standard Sermons,* 2:390-91.

[48]Wesley, *Works,* 12:257.

[49]Ibid., 12:207.

[50]John Skinner, *Genesis,* The International Critical Commentary (Edinburgh: T. & T. Clark, 1963), p. 290.

[51]*The Letters of John Wesley,* 2:280.

[52]E. Stanley Jones, *Abundant Living* (Nashville: Abingdon, 1980), p. 153.

A Lutheran Response
Gerhard O. Forde

*L*AURENCE WOOD'S PRESENTATION OF THE WESLEYAN PERSPEC-
tive gives us an almost classic example of the difficulties in
attempting to describe sanctification in a fashion urgent
enough to spur Christians on, yet without somehow denigrating the
gift given in Christ. For Wood, in the manner of Wesley, sanctification
is described as a *process,* a matter of becoming "in reality" what is given
in Christ through the new birth. It is a "dialectic movement" in which
Christ's pure love *becomes* an "inner reality," a "continuous happening"
through the indwelling of the Spirit. The goal of the process, following
Wesley, is Christian perfection—a particular kind of perfection, carefully nuanced indeed, but nevertheless fostering a system which causes
all the mischief.

As in the other essays, one may once again find the description of
sanctification and its aims helpful, but the use, the implementation of
it, wanting. The description of sanctification as a process leads to the
temptation to make the process itself into the basic theological scheme.
The difficulty with all such ordinary process thinking theologically is
that it just doesn't work with a grace that is given totally and freely at
the outset. "Progress" according to the process means that previous
advents of grace or previous accomplishments seem somehow *less* than

subsequent ones. Each step in the process appears more or less a staging platform for subsequent "bigger and better" steps. The unconditional grace of God just doesn't fit such schemes and tends to be minimized if not lost altogether.

No matter how strenuously one denies it in theory, it is impossible to prevent such schemes from becoming a kind of "practical Pelagianism," wherein original sin does not exist and sanctification is gained by our exercise of free will. To begin with, understanding sanctification as a process of becoming holy makes holiness into a moral quality. Furthermore, since it is to be attained by a process, I am then bidden to look to myself to see "how I am doing," how "holy" I am becoming. Where I meet with something less than success I can only lay the blame on myself. It must be just because I have not tried hard enough to reach the desired goal. At this point the theologian or pastor may protest that grace is free, absolutely free, and that all I have to do is to "let Jesus or grace or God into my life," or something like that. But that only makes matters worse. Grace is absolutely free. God has done everything to make it so. But then why doesn't it work? It can only be because I have not "let it in," or made the proper decision, or gotten some kind of a "leg up on the process." The more one talks *about* free grace when one thinks in terms of such a process, the worse it gets. Since grace is free, then *everything* will depend on whatever little bit it is that I am supposed to contribute to the process. The result is always practical pelagianism.

Grace simply cannot be put together with such process thinking without being generally eclipsed by the scheme. No matter how much one talks about free grace, it turns out to be only theory—what has been dubbed an "anti-Pelagian codicil"—which is ultimately displaced by the "reality" of the process. Perhaps at best grace functions as a kind of "temporary loan" which covers you until you actually "earn" your holiness. In Wood's words, you become "in reality" what you "already are." The language itself seems to imply that what you are by grace is something less than the "reality" finally to be delivered by the process. In the zeal to describe sanctification as a realizable process, the language itself simply leads us into one trap after another. But that is the way the tyranny of "the law" works.

Wood's essay on the Wesleyan perspective struggles heroically with the difficulties of trying to put the free grace of new birth together with a process idea of sanctification. But in spite of its many fine points the essay does not succeed in overcoming the difficulties.

The most attractive aspect of the Wesleyan perspective is that it does hold out for an *expectation*—a real hope for fulfillment, even for "perfection." Indeed, the expectation is the decisive thing, Wood insists. It is of course the temptation of those who deny ideas of process to fall off the stool on the other side and imply that nothing at all happens after the absolute gift of free grace. Then there is no hope, no expectation at all. That would be equally misleading. That would be like saying that nothing at all happens after the beloved's unconditional "I love you." The subtle and difficult thing in our talk about growth or progress in sanctification is that it absolutely must be presented not as *our* progress toward the goal, but rather just the opposite: *the goal's moving more and more in upon us and possessing us.* In that sense the expectation is the decisive thing. It is, indeed, the *whole* thing. That is why I think it necessary to say that whatever we mean by sanctification is just the art of "getting used to" justification. It is the life "breathed into us" by the Holy Spirit, the sanctifier. Whatever moral progress cajoled out of us by the various artifices of the law cannot qualify as sanctification.

Even though the Wesleyan perspective breathes much evangelical fervor, it seems always to be halting between a dedication to the free grace of God in Jesus Christ, on the one hand, and its zeal for moral progress, on the other. The main scheme it seems to settle on to resolve its divided allegiance is a kind of "two stage" theory of grace. Thus Wood's presentation abounds in terminology which tries to recognize the essential importance of the "first" advent of grace, at the same time as it wants to insist on a "second" blessing, or rest, or gift—an "entire" sanctification, a "deeper" Christian life, which, supposedly, does not minimize the reception of Christ in conversion, and so on. This is all backed up biblically by a kind of typological exegesis which draws on the different stages in the history of salvation (exodus/conquest) and even on a supposed two-stage dispensation of Christ and Spirit drawn from the New Testament, including the incidents in Acts 8:14-17 and 19:1-7 where baptism and the gift of the Spirit are separated by an interval of time. Incidentally with regard to the latter, it seems questionable to draw dogmatic conclusion from what was considered even in Acts to be highly irregular, if not a kind of miscarriage. The disciples did not *approve* of the separation between baptism and the Spirit. They apparently thought it unusual and took steps to remedy the matter. It therefore seems unreasonable to draw on such incidents to support a two-stage theory of grace.

The two-stage theory of grace does not escape the perils of attempting to combine the unconditional grace of God with thinking in terms of ordinary human schemes of progress and process. If the grace is given freely and unconditionally it means the end of all such schemes. If the scheme is retained it tends always to eclipse grace or relegate it to secondary status. The attempt to retain both usually ends in a precarious sort of balancing act in which one tries not to overemphasize one aspect at the expense of the other, but then tends to lose the power of both. So one must not assume that everything is given with the first grace, on the one hand, at the same time as one must not overdo the claims of perfection, on the other. One ends by halting between "stages."

The typological exegesis also creates difficulties. To be sure, it is not "allegorical," but it is more like the old tropological exegesis which sought to extract the moral meaning (the meaning for existence, in today's jargon) from the literal history. As such, it too was intrinsically Pelagian. The text no longer functions to end the old and raise up the new; it merely informs or tells *about* what one is to do. In other words, the Word is no longer the sword of the Spirit which sanctifies through its power to kill and make alive; it merely tells *about* sanctification under the more-or-less-hidden form of historical types to which we must then subsequently relate as best we can. Wood is right in seeing that we are not to take biblical history merely in a "static and rationalistic" sense. But typological tropology won't do either.

The Word does not merely tell *about* sanctification; it sanctifies through its power to end the old and raise up the new. The history, the long struggle of God with his people, spells one thing for the old Adam and Eve: death. And then it raises up the new. That is how sanctification occurs. And if we are to speak rightly of these matters, we must do so in a way that fosters a sanctifying use of the Word.

By merit alone men advance in holiness.

A Reformed Response
Sinclair B. Ferguson

THE STORY OF JOHN WESLEY'S PILGRIMAGE TO FAITH PLAYED A role in my own Christian beginnings as a teen-ager. I therefore appreciate Dr. Wood's concern to interpret the Wesleys' teaching on Christian perfection on its own terms, and to seek to safeguard it from misunderstanding. I also appreciate Dr. Wood's concern to root his exposition of this doctrine in biblical theology and not merely in experience or church tradition. Furthermore, I am impressed by the positive, upbeat note in the Wesleyan doctrine of sanctification. It is all too easy to excuse our little progress in holiness and love on the basis of the continuing power of indwelling sin and to play down the biblical emphasis on the new creation (2 Cor 5:17). Perhaps there is a special temptation for Reformed Christians to make their emphasis on the cognitive a refuge from the inbreaking of God's Spirit which floods our hearts with the love of God, joy unspeakable that is already full of glory.

Despite my appreciation, however, there are several points at which the Wesleyan view and the Reformed view differ.

First, "Perfect love drives out fear" (1 Jn 4:18). Here, "perfect" does not carry the same connotation as its modern English usage. Perfection in the New Testament normally denotes maturity. Mature love delivers us from the ghost of our guilty fears because it is related to a new and different view of God's judgment of us (see 2 Tim 4:8). In addition, this "perfect love" is not viewed as an isolatable experience. At no point does John suggest that it is "received" in some instantaneous experience.

In this connection it is noteworthy that the early Wesleyan testimonies to receiving "perfect love" seem to focus on what was felt. Since "love drives out fear" (1 Jn 4:18), one wonders whether the experience they cherished would have been better described as deliverance from fear. That certainly would have been less open to misunderstanding.

Second, although Paul does speak about being sanctified "through and through" (1 Thess 5:23-24), he does not regard this as an experience to be received by a specific act of faith. Rather it seems to be the consummation of the ongoing work of God's Spirit. It is God putting the finishing touches to the work he has already begun in us (Phil 1:6). In common with many other traditions of exegesis, Reformed thought takes the reference in 1 Thessalonians 5:23-24 to point to the consummation of sanctification at the return of Christ. That is underlined by Paul's stated concern here for the complete sanctification of *the body*, which surely has the resurrection in view (see also Rom 8:23).

Third, Wesley found it necessary to qualify his teaching to guard it from obvious misunderstanding. So he taught that perfect love does not deliver us from all sin, but only from conscious, willful transgression. But the one passage in Scripture which speaks about the Christian as one who "cannot go on sinning" (1 Jn 3:9), which Dr. Wood exegetes in terms of John's definition of sin as "lawlessness" (1 Jn 3:4), cannot refer to some Christians only. For John is here describing what is true of all Christians. Those who do not sin or do not continue in sin are not a limited group of Christians who have received perfect love or Christian perfection by faith. They are all those who have been born of God, or all Christians. These statements cannot therefore be made to support a view that distinguishes among Christians into those who have, and those who have not, experienced perfect love.

If John Wesley did not belong to those who "cannot go on sinning" (whatever the interpretation of 1 John 3), his deficiency would not have been in perfect love, Christian perfection or entire sanctification,

PT. Wesleyan view says there are two
stages in sanctification
— NOT } experienced } 125 Not
— HAVE } perfect love } → sinning
consciously

A REFORMED RESPONSE

but it would have been a deficiency of regeneration! To use this passage in any way to undergird two stages of spiritual experience is self-defeating precisely because it is a universal description of Christians as regenerate.

Fourth, Wesley's distinction between conscious, willful sin and other sin does not seem to Reformed theology to square with the New Testament's perception of sin as propensity and sin as act, intimately related as cause and effect. The Old Testament distinction between conscious sin and unwitting sin seems to me to refer to something quite different and has specific reference to the period of the Mosaic ordinances. According to the New Testament we are totally responsible for sin as propensity and for sin as specific action.

It is noticeable in Wesley's writings on Christian perfection that in order to defend this doctrine he found it necessary virtually to regard the apostles (unlike himself) as sinless in the sense of experiencing Christian perfection. (Compare Dr. Wood's understanding of 1 Corinthians 4:4, which Reformed exegesis, by contrast, takes to be a general claim to right dealings, rather than one of perfection. See also Paul's denial of his own perfection in Philippians 3:12.)

Related to this is the fact that Wesley did not believe that Romans 7:14-25 described mature Christian experience. By contrast, even those Reformed exegetes who deny that this passage refers to Paul the Christian do not deny that the mature Christian inevitably struggles with indwelling sin (see Gal 5:17). The sharpness of the tension between salvation already begun and salvation not yet consummated should never be downplayed. But Wesley seems to me to so downplay it. As in his gospel proclamation, Wesley held that responsibility to believe in Christ assumed ability to believe (contrary to his Reformed colleague George Whitefield), and so in sanctification he seems to have assumed that the desire to experience perfection assumed the ability to experience it now. In both of these areas, Whitefield believed Wesley was mistaken, and his Reformed teaching reflected those differences.

For all the clearing away of misunderstandings, Wesley's view seems to Reformed theology to represent a less than biblical view of sin. Every Reformed theologian would want to say to those who claim to experience freedom from conscious sin: "You have not yet considered how great the weight of sin is" (Anselm of Canterbury).

One final problem remains. How does a Reformed Christian respond to the stubborn insistence by many Methodists (and others) that they have experienced Christian perfection? B. B. Warfield's answer earlier this century was that it was not love, but peace, that they have experienced. My own answer would be along slightly different lines: Christians of many traditions have experienced the fulfillment of Christ's promise to reveal himself to them through his Word and Spirit. Reformed Christians like John Owen, George Whitefield and Jonathan Edwards have borne witness in different ways to the powerful testimony of God's Spirit in their lives, flooding their hearts with love, assurance and compassion for others. Thomas Chalmers, for example, spoke of "the expulsive power of a new affection."

It is possible to be delivered from "a spirit that makes you a slave again to fear" (Rom 8:15). The love of God, poured out into our hearts, has this effect (Rom 5:5), teaching us to rejoice in God, in our present sufferings and in the hope of glory (Rom 5:2-3, 11). Reformed theology does not necessarily deny the reality of the experience of many Wesleyans. It holds, however, that Wesley and his disciples gave this experience the wrong name and, as a result, misinterpreted its significance—sometimes with unhappy consequences for themselves and others who followed them.

Happily, with the Wesleys and with Wesleyans, Reformed Christians also sing:

O grant that nothing in my soul
May dwell but thy pure love alone.

But Reformed Christians do not expect to experience the complete answer to that prayer until they see Christ face to face and are made like him. Then, thankfully, our differences will be no more!

A Pentecostal Response
Russell P. Spittler

WESLEYANS PURSUE HOLINESS. PENTECOSTALS SEEK THE BAP-
tism in the Holy Spirit. The Reformed tradition describes
sanctification as a sort of salvific gradualism. And the
Lutheran tradition virtually makes of sanctification a reverse image to
justification, while the contemplative view describes a mystic interiority
found by a few. But all of these affirm growth in Christian character
and values. Whatever other lessons emerge from these pages, thought-
ful Christians may well come to appreciate the varieties of the quest.

Pentecostals in lifestyle and doctrine lie closer to Wesleyan values,
for the most part, than to the other traditions listed above. Like Wesleyans, Pentecostals highly value experience. And they too allow that
substantial Christian advance may rise from what Princeton's James
Loder calls a "transforming moment"—regardless of how that moment
is titled or theologized. Methodism presents a classic fourfold scaffold
of authority that Pentecostals could easily absorb—the Bible, Christian
experience, tradition (a prominent, but largely unacknowledged force
in Pentecostalism) and reason.

Even Reformed Pentecostals have used the term "entire sanctification." But the adjective was dropped from the doctrinal statement of
the Assemblies of God in 1961, perhaps as a way to reduce needless

confusion with the Wesleyan Pentecostals.

The two traditions are alike in still another way: they must devise intricate arguments to explain their distinctive doctrines. Wesleyans speak of perfect love, yet they say they don't intend to imply flawlessness or sinlessness. Pentecostals, by affirming speaking in tongues as the necessary initial physical evidence of the baptism in the Holy Spirit, create the impression, according to their critics, that believers who don't speak in tongues are "second class citizens." Extracting such implications may seem logical, but they do not reflect the intentions of those who framed the imperfect statements. And intentionality, common evangelical wisdom has it, should always guide interpretation.

Mr. Wood's exodus/conquest typology—prefiguring resurrection/Pentecost, both for Christ and for his individual followers—is a helpful one. But what of the wandering and the wilderness between? Surely the years spent there bespeak the course of the Christian's pilgrimage—zigzagging along between we're-not-what-we-used-to-be and we're-not-yet-what-we're-going-to-be. Is sanctification the route that links the exodus and the conquest?

↳ Good point!

A Contemplative Response
E. Glenn Hinson

THIS ESSAY APPEARS TO GIVE AN ADEQUATE EXPOSITION OF THE Wesleyan *theory* of sanctification, but severely shortchanges the aspect of sanctification for which John Wesley showed the greatest genius, namely, its implementation among the working masses who felt alienated from the church. Although it is important to know the theological underpinnings of this significant tradition, theology must prove itself in practice, in the kind of lives it inspires in those who adhere to its certain set of beliefs. Wesleyan thought has always come out better in practice than in theory.

Much in Wesley's view of sanctification is in harmony with the contemplative tradition, probably by design. Both certainly would give preference to an existential rather than a rationalistic approach to the Scriptures. Both would view sanctification as a process whereby the love of Christ becomes a reality in the inner person. Confusion in or about the way in which Wesley viewed sanctification—whether progressive or "entire"—replicates a debate long present in the contemplative tradition, just like the saints of an earlier day. Wesley too realized that all growth in love depends on grace. If he did indeed espouse the idea of "perfection in love" as attainable in this life, however, he went beyond most of the great spiritual guides, such as Bernard of Clairvaux. Bernard doubted whether even martyrs achieved the fourth stage of love (love of self for God's sake) here and now. On that point Bernard may have been more realistic than Wesley on the basis of experience, testimonies notwithstanding.

Splits in Methodism that produced the holiness and Pentecostal movements prove how confusing Wesley's thought could be on the doctrine of perfection. "Perfection" is itself a heavy concept to place on the shoulders of those who, in ordinary life, salute it from afar. That is why the Catholic tradition of spirituality (shaped especially by Augustine) and the Lutheran and Reformed traditions steered toward the apostle Paul, rather than toward the Johannine letters. The danger Augustine spied in Pelagianism, the Reformers also saw in medieval Catholicism and Calvinists in Arminianism—a tendency to raise expectations so high only an elite could attain it, thus adding to human insecurity. It is good, therefore, to hear that Wesley did not interpret "perfection in love" as "sinless perfection." Yet the two regularly have gotten confused in the holiness and Pentecostal traditions. I wonder, therefore, whether the term "perfection" shouldn't be dropped. The Greek word *teleios* seldom appears in the New Testament, nor do its cognates, and it does not mean what most persons associate today with the word *perfection*. The same is true of the idea of "entire sanctification." Anytime we have to spend so much energy clarifying and defining concepts, wouldn't it be better to find different terms to express what we want to say?

The Pentecostal wing emerging out of the Methodist tradition has recovered a theological accent often neglected in Christian history vis-à-vis the role of the Spirit in Christian life. Like all reform movements, this one too may have overstressed extraordinary phenomena such as tongues-speaking or healing as evidences of the Spirit to the neglect of others, such as the virtues of love, joy, peace (Gal 5:22) and Christian unity (1 Cor 12—14). Yet somewhere within the body of Christ there has been a need for an unmistakable accent to offer a counterweight. The modern charismatic movement has revitalized many of the mainline churches. The Pentecostal tradition, however, does suffer from deficiencies that may be rooted in what the author calls "dispensational exposition of Christian experience." Can we divide history so neatly into dispensations? To a degree perhaps, but we must be careful we do not forfeit a balanced trinitarian theology wherein we confess God as Father, Son and Spirit at one and the same time and not successively—now the Father (Old Testament), now the Son (in the Incarnation) and now the Spirit (after the resurrection).

The author has developed well two themes of the Wesleyan tradition, elucidating the biblical foundation for each. Curiously, he has expended more space on the idea of "Pentecostal grace" emphasized by Wesley's early disciple John Fletcher than he has on Wesley's own favorite theme of "circumcision of the heart." He has sustained and explained both ideas, however, by solid biblical exposition. Especially interesting, by way of contrast with the Lutheran paper, is an argument drawn from Rudolf Bultmann, a Lutheran, that Paul emphasized sanctification ("freedom from sin") rather than justification ("forgiveness of sins")! Here would have been a perfect spot to bring in Wesley's practical insights on spiritual formation. How do we tap into the Holy Spirit's sanctifying efforts? Can we assume this will happen if we "wait on the Spirit"? Or do we need to prepare ourselves by intense and persistent prayer, worship, spiritual guidance and other activities?

The Pentecostal View
Russell P. Spittler

FIVE *BILLION PEOPLE LIVE ON THE GLOBE AT THIS POINT IN*
the century. Of these a third—1.6 billion—profess to be Christians. And of the Christians, well above half, some 906 million,
are found in the Roman Catholic Church. There are, however, only
slightly more than a third as many Protestants as there are Roman
Catholics: 305 million Protestants in all (not counting 52 million Anglicans, who in principle eschew classification as Protestants).

Demographics of Pentecostalism

Already in 1982, when David B. Barrett's *World Christian Encyclopedia*
was published, it had become clear that Pentecostals and charismatics
formed the single largest sector of Protestantism.[1] But projections for
mid-1988 yield 333,000,000 Pentecostal/charismatics worldwide—
21.4% of the world's known church members.[2]

Pentecostal spirituality therefore has quietly emerged as the new
majority Protestant spirituality—a status equally unrealized by the
movement itself and by the Christian church at large, except for the
scholarly informed. And when the total figures are combined for classical Pentecostals along with charismatics from Anglican, Orthodox,
Roman Catholic and mainline Protestant sectors, the sum exceeds the

size of Protestantism as a whole. If for no other reason than statistical dominance, the spirituality of Pentecostalism calls for analysis.

But who are the Pentecostals, the charismatics? This widely diverse cluster of Christians ranges from Appalachian snake-handlers gathered in rustic mountain churches to multimillion-dollar urban megachurches having multiple ministerial staffs in receipt, not uncommonly, of six-figure salaries. The movement varies: a red-brick, unadorned church of two hundred in rural Pennsylvania; a hastily renovated former supermarket in Orange County, California; a theme park in South Carolina; a prayer tower centerpiece amid a major university campus in Oklahoma; nursing mothers, pickup trucks and blue collars in the rural South; yuppies with TransAms in the concrete centers of commerce; yelling preachers on early Sunday-morning television; but also a German tent-evangelist drawing scores of thousands to high-energy revival meetings in Africa; a hospital in Bangalore; an orphanage in Egypt; a leprosarium on Africa's west coast; a daily newspaper in Norway; Christian day-schools crafted from leased surplus school buildings in Michigan; guitars and raised hands at a Catholic mass. These all are Pentecostal or charismatic.

Pentecostal Origins and Emphases

If some varieties of Christians are geographically uniform and predictable, Pentecostals are neither. Certain features nearly always occur, yet the variety is astonishing.

Who are the Pentecostals, the charismatics? How do the two differ? Some distinctions are in order.

Pentecostals and charismatics of every variety are distinguished by their emphasis on the Holy Spirit and their beliefs in the contemporary relevance of the gifts of the Spirit. As a whole, they all reflect a conservative Christian orthodoxy (though a nontrinitarian variety will be mentioned). They value personal religious renewal. They reflect a restorationist impulse, a bent to an often idealized "church of the New Testament." But there the similarities end.

Pentecostals stemmed from the decades that flanked the birth of the twentieth century. They emerged largely, though not entirely, from the holiness churches of the nineteenth century—revivalist groups of mainly Wesleyan origin, which sought personal and ecclesiastical renewal through the pursuit of something more in the Christian life, after-burner experiences variously called "perfect love," "Christian perfec-tion," "sanctification" and eventually the "baptism in the Holy Spirit."[3]

What decisively marked off the Pentecostals from the holiness bodies was the acceptance of speaking in tongues as a legitimate, and even necessary, variety of Christian experience. Though in the last quarter of the nineteenth century various holiness groups were teaching and experiencing the baptism in the Holy Spirit, it was the Pentecostal insistence on speaking in tongues as the "initial physical evidence" of this baptism that gave birth to the Pentecostal movement. Other spir-itual gifts such as healing were endorsed by the neighbor churches of the early Pentecostals.

Perhaps because of its very physiological specificity, speaking in tongues has become more or less a touchstone by which Pentecostals, and charismatics as well, can be identified. Since a distinguishing char-acteristic in popular usage readily gets confused with an essential qual-ity, both Pentecostalism and charismatics have been pejoratively re-ferred to as a "Tongues Movement." Precise historical origins wear smooth over time, and the world today can speak easily of Quakers, Baptists and Methodists with little consciousness of the shaking, dip-ping and systematizing that spawned those originally pejorative terms.

However, not all Pentecostals around the world do, nor in their origins did, teach that speaking in tongues is the *necessary* initial phys-ical evidence of the baptism in the Holy Spirit. A large majority of contemporary charismatics do not affirm the necessity of tongues; in-deed, that hesitance among charismatics is one of the principal features that distinguishes them from Pentecostals. Most Scandinavian, some German and a few South American classical Pentecostal groups stop short of the insistence on tongues as initial evidence, which is a fun-damental belief of the Pentecostal Fellowship of North America (PFNA), the primary ecumenical cluster of the Pentecostal established denominations.

Varieties of Classical Pentecostalism

Benedictine scholar Kilian McDonnell, an astute analyst of this relig-ious family, coined the term "classical Pentecostalism" to refer to those groups that formed around the turn of the century. Something of a historical miscarriage produced the Pentecostal churches. Without the tolerance that marked the irenic ecumenical environment that followed World War 2, newly Spirit-baptized holiness Christians found scant welcome in their home churches—except when the entire church adopted Pentecostal teachings. Eventually this led to the formation of Pentecostal denominations, at times along geographical lines or owing to twice-charismatic leadership (charismatic in personality and theology).

The oldest form of classical Pentecostalism, what can be called a *Wesleyan* variety, clung steadfastly to its established notion of sanctification as a "second definite work"—a post-conversional, cleansing experience that enhanced personal holiness and, according to some, radically removed the bent to sin. In these groups the baptism in the Holy Spirit, accompanied by speaking in tongues, became a third distinct experience for Christians—following conversion and sanctification. This baptism provided not personal holiness but empowerment for Christian service such as missionary evangelism or pastoral leadership. Surviving examples of such churches include the Church of God (Cleveland, Tennessee), the Pentecostal Holiness Church and the Church of God in Christ.

Mainly through the teachings of William Durham, an early twentieth-century Chicago pastor who emphasized the "finished work of Christ," and whose religious background did not include the holiness tradition, a second variety of Pentecostalism emerged—*Baptistic* or *Reformed* Pentecostalism. In effect, Durham merged into one the two "subsequent" experiences distinguished by holiness Pentecostals—that is, sanctification and the baptism in the Holy Spirit. This now *second* work of the Spirit was called the baptism in the Holy Spirit: sanctification by this sector of Pentecostals was viewed along Reformed lines, progressing from conversion to death (or to the Second Coming, whichever was to come first). Examples of this group are the International Church of the Foursquare Gospel, the Assemblies of God and the Open Bible Standard Churches.

A third species of classical Pentecostalism arose in 1916. At the second general council of the young Assemblies of God, which was founded only two years earlier with the ideal of avoiding any doctrinal statement, a clarifying trinitarian statement was issued. That action was necessitated to quell a burgeoning teaching that illustrates a character-istic Pentecostal bent for literal biblical interpretation. At a camp meet-ing between Los Angeles and Pasadena, one John Scheppe concluded a new baptismal formula, "In the name of Jesus, only," from a reading of the book of Acts—which everywhere states that persons were bap-tized "in the name of Jesus" and nowhere uses the trinitarian formu-lation of Matthew 28:19. At a period in its infancy, some important leaders in early Pentecostalism accepted rebaptism—this time "in the name of Jesus." A theology emerged which taught that God's name is Jesus, that Jesus alone is God, that Father and Spirit are merely titles or aspects of Jesus. This part of Pentecostalism has been described as a sort of "unitarianism in reverse," a unitarianism of the second person of the trinity. The largest group preserving this teaching is the United Pentecostal Church. Another is the Pentecostal Assemblies of the World. These *"Jesus Name"* or *unitarian* Pentecostals are shunned by the establishment Pentecostals represented in the PFNA, from which they are excluded. But the teaching flourishes in Indonesia and certain parts of African Pentecostalism and elsewhere in the Third World.

Neo-Pentecostalism, the Charismatic Movement

The relationship between Pentecostalism and the charismatic move-ment resembles that between an airplane and a helicopter. Both gener-ally do the same thing. There are more similarities than differences. Though certain features are shared, distinctive characteristics apply. And the one could not have developed had not the other first existed.

Through the first half of the twentieth century, Pentecostalism grew steadily. Opposed by fundamentalists, especially in the second and third decades, American Pentecostals nevertheless acquired doctrinal features of that movement (Scofieldian dispensationalism, for example) and adopted its mores.

Following World War 2, however, Pentecostalism moved across the tracks. Rebirth of the fundamentalist movement into what might be called "Wheaton evangelicalism" yielded a more tolerant theological environment whose new leaders allowed the notable evangelistic and missionary exploits of the Pentecostals to compensate for the perceived curious notions about the Holy Spirit held by Pentecostals. By 1960, the chief executive officer of the Assemblies of God was voted in as the president of the National Association of Evangelicals.

But 1960 was also the year when Dennis Bennett, an Episcopal rector serving in Van Nuys, California, announced that he too had personally experienced the baptism of the Holy Spirit. The next year, 1961, the Assemblies of God began actions which resulted in the withdrawal (in 1962) of the ministerial credentials of David du Plessis— roving interpreter of the Pentecostal experience. Du Plessis's trips to Yale, Princeton, the Riverside Drive precincts of the National Council of Churches, World Council of Churches circles in Geneva and his meetings with highly placed Roman Catholics proved embarrassing to the newly achieved evangelical status of his church. Though there were others who preceded them, Bennett and du Plessis can be reckoned as the progenitors of the charismatic movement.

Bennett never left the Episcopal Church. David du Plessis is widely and gratefully remembered for his counsel to the newly Spirit-baptized to stay in their own churches. Indeed, this impulse—couched in irenic postwar ecumenism—indelibly distinguished Pentecostalism from its daughter movement. Pentecostals bolted and formed their own denominations, while charismatics stayed in their own mainstream churches and organized denominationally specific "charismatic service agencies."

By the end of the sixties, charismatic spirituality had emerged even in the Roman Catholic Church. In a few conspicuous cases, the charismatic threat wrenched a local Protestant congregation from its denominational moorings. Hence there exist today independent charismatic churches, some of which present a configuration of beliefs and practices not easy to parallel elsewhere among charismatics or Pentecostals.

By far the bulk of the charismatic movement lies as a spread over the existing denominational map. Nearly all major sectors of Christendom include congregations, or subgroups within parishes, who believe and practice Pentecostal piety. Yet they have not left the church. Organized national service offices in good standing with their parent denominations today exist to serve the Presbyterian and Reformed Churches, Methodists, Episcopalians, Lutherans, Greek Orthodox, Roman Catholics, Mennonites, the United Church of Christ and others. Such efforts are least successful where there exists theological proximity to

Pentecostalism, coupled with early historical rejection of Pentecostal emphases. A group aiming to serve Wesleyan Methodists and members of the Church of the Nazarene, for example, understandably enjoys no official welcome.

Varieties of Charismatics

With the penetration of Pentecostal values, beliefs and practices into mainstream Christianity, considerably less theological or ecclesiastical uniformity can be affirmed of the charismatic movement than can be asserted of classical Pentecostalism as a whole. Roman Catholic charismatics, for example, show a sturdy loyalty to their church, and they are officially accommodated by the hierarchy.[4] Though Roman theologians still attach being "born again" to the sacrament of baptism (usually of infants), lay charismatic Catholics renewed by the Pentecostal baptism will speak of "coming to know the Lord personally" while competent charismatic Roman Catholic theologians speak more readily of the baptism in the Spirit as a "release of the Spirit." Thus, charismatic theology accommodates to its specific ecclesiastical environment.

Roman Catholics and Lutherans—both groups have sturdy academic traditions—have taken the lead in fashioning charismatic theology. Classical Pentecostals, having revivalist origins, to this day are strongly influenced by anti-intellectual assumptions and hence have produced little substantial published theology. But that is changing.

In summary, Pentecostalism arose early in the first half of this century, charismatics in the second half. Pentecostals formed the classical Pentecostal denominations; charismatics remained in their own churches, the mainstream ones. Most (though not all) Pentecostals insist on tongues as initial evidence; charismatics generally speak in tongues but do not make it a matter of necessity. Pentecostals teach a strict subsequence of vital Christian experiences—two in the case of Baptistic Pentecostals and three in Wesleyan Pentecostalism. Charismatics, on the other hand, find ways to fit charismatic experience and renewal into their existing ecclesiastical and theological traditions. Pentecostals, at least the North American varieties, are likely to reflect the rigoristic mores rising from their holiness origins and fundamentalist encounter; charismatics might smoke pipes or attend dances, depending on their church customs. Pentecostals have longstanding institutions—denominational headquarters, schools, orphanages and skid-row missions, for example. Charismatics are sociologically less developed as a movement, and their institutions consist of newer independent congregations, recently established magazines or ministries, and charismatic service agencies in good standing with mainstream church headquarters.

These differences, here only sketched, make for different spiritualities. But now it is important to see how the word *spirituality* is understood in the context of the Pentecostal and charismatic movements.

What Is Spirituality?

At least two nuances of the word *spirituality* must be distinguished.[5] Since the early 1890s, the word *spirituality* has been used in the sociology of religion to describe that cluster of religious practices which express the beliefs and values of a particular religious group. In this sense, the term is roughly similar to earlier technical words like *religio, pietas, eusebia, leiturgia*—even *Euthusiasmus*. In this sense the word is scientifically neutral. Apart from the traditional varieties of Christian spiritualities, one could speak of Mormon, Islamic or Buddhist spirituality.

It is important to understand that *spirituality* in this sociological sense is not native to the vocabulary of Pentecostalism, even though the word finds limited use among a few emerging scholars of that tradition. Far more frequent, in fact, is the adjective *spiritual. Spirituality,* in ordinary use among Pentecostals, refers to the personal or individual quality of being spiritual. And *spiritual* describes a committed believer who is perceived to be, to use the tradition's own jargon, open to the things of the Spirit, fully consecrated to God, endowed perhaps with one or two spiritual gifts besides speaking in tongues (which would be assumed)—perhaps the gifts of healing, knowledge, discernment of spirits or wisdom. *Spiritual,* in other words, within Pentecostalism goes roughly for what would usually be called "religious" outside the movement.

In any case, "being spiritual" or "spirituality" in Pentecostal usage refers to a *personal quality* of an individual person, lay or clerical. Charismatic usage of the term cannot be separately tracked, because today's

charismatics became so as adults—the movement is that young. Just
how charismatics in any of the streams of Christendom define the term
spirituality will depend on the impact of the ecclesiastical tradition in
which they were formed. Some contemporary charismatics uncritically
adopt the Pentecostal nuance of the term.

This Pentecostal nuance of the term *spirituality* refers to a quality of
individual piety that admits of degrees (as in, "more spiritual," "concerned over the weakness of her spirituality"). Such language reveals
two features of Pentecostalism: its high value on individualism and its
largely nonscientific outlook.

What is discussed in this chapter represents an inquiry that Pentecostalism would hardly think to do of itself. Most Pentecostal devotees
would expect this inquiry to be an assessment of the spiritual health
of the movement. It is not movements, in Pentecostal understanding,
but individual persons that make up movements who have "spirituality."

Nevertheless, this essay joins these rarely linked terms and, in what
follows, provides an index of the practices and styles of classical Pentecostals sufficiently comprehensive to delineate—in keeping with the
theme of this book—a Pentecostal spirituality. Because of the recency,
diversity and differences of the charismatic movement, no systematic
effort is made here to describe a separate charismatic spirituality. Nor
should it be assumed that whatever is Pentecostal is also charismatic—
or vice versa. Yet distinguishable aspects of charismatic spirituality will
be mentioned in the context of the related feature of the mother movement, Pentecostalism.

The Place of Experience in Pentecostalism

Though it may seem awkward to identify individual experience as a
dimension of spirituality, the spirituality of Pentecostalism cannot be
grasped without comprehending the lofty role of personal religious
experience among Pentecostals. Individualism, long identified as a
mark of revivalist sects and often deplored within enlightened religious
circles, is clearly a virtue among Pentecostals.

Like their evangelical neighbors, they will call upon men and women
everywhere to "accept Jesus as their personal Savior." But unlike evangelicals, they will in addition urge believers earnestly to seek the bap-

tism in the Holy Spirit. This Spirit baptism is, in Pentecostal understanding, known to have occurred when the baptized believer speaks
in tongues. Since glossolalia rises from a single human pharynx, Pentecostal spirituality places highly specific demands on personal religious experience. One cannot be a Pentecostal without having had the
Pentecostal experience—a personalized repetition of the baptizing
work of the Spirit mentioned in Acts 2, 10, 19 and 2 Corinthians 12
(as Pentecostals interpret these passages).

To understand this high regard for experience held by Pentecostals,
it may be helpful to recall the taxonomy outlined in Lesslie Newbigin's
classic book *The Household of God*.[6] In that work, which predated the
rise of the charismatic movement, the then-bishop of the church of
South India identified three major approaches to Christianity—the
Catholic, the Protestant and the Pentecostal. Newbigin used the terms
in a generic sense so that "Catholic" included not only Roman Catholics but Anglicans and others in the broad "Catholic" tradition. Likewise, it is fair to note, Newbigin did not intend to limit his use of the
term "Pentecostal" to what is now called the classical Pentecostal movement. But the historic Pentecostals certainly belong in Newbigin's cate-
gory which bears their name.

According to Newbigin, Protestants define the church as the congregation of the faithful—orthodoxy is central. Catholics view the
church as sacramental incorporation into the body of Christ—obedient
participation within an acknowledged historic and visible structure is
fundamental. And Pentecostals think of the church as the fellowship
of the Holy Spirit—and experience is pivotal.[7] Each of these represents
an avenue of approach to God—all legitimately Christian, but each
palpably diverse. And of course features of each spill over into any one
of the three ecclesiologies.

Pentecostal Obedience

Of course Bishop Newbigin's categories of Catholic obedience and
Protestant orthodoxy appear as well in Pentecostalism. Obedience
thrives as a motif of its hymnody (for instance, "Trust and obey, for
there's no other way") and sometimes has led to a legalistic type of piety
configured along the lines of rigoristic ethics: avoid theaters, dances,
gambling, smoking, drinking and—in earlier days and in more rural

sites—things like mixed bathing (women and men swimming together), drinking Coke, caffeinated beverages, playing ball on Sundays and the like.

Of course when Roman Catholics become Pentecostal, clear aspects of obedience arise. One manifestation is that Catholic Pentecostal prayer groups usually insist on a priest being present, and they brandish a firm loyalty to the local parish as well as papal structures and procedures.

Even if local examples of rural legalism can still be found, it is inaccurate to portray the core of Pentecostalism as a concern for obedience within a sacramental structure. (In fact, Pentecostals are uncomfortable in the presence of sacramentalism.) Experience, rather, occupies the quintessential place.

Pentecostal Orthodoxy

Orthodoxy also characterizes Pentecostalism. But that trait is a latecomer. When, for example, the Assemblies of God was formed in 1914, no doctrinal statement was proposed. To the contrary, its preamble and resolution of constitution contained this paragraph:

> WHEREAS, We recognize ourselves as members of said GENERAL ASSEMBLY OF GOD (which is God's organism), and do not believe in identifying ourselves as, or establishing ourselves into, a sect, that is a human organization that legislates or forms laws and articles of faith and has unscriptural jurisdiction over members and creates unscriptural lines of fellowship and disfellowship and which separates itself from other members of the General Assembly (Church) of the first born, which is contrary to Christ's prayer in St. John 17, and Paul's teaching in Eph. 4:1-16, which we heartily endorse. . . .[8]

Yet only two years later a minimal doctrinal statement was hastily assembled when the common trinitarian assumptions of the young church were imperiled by what became known as the "Jesus Name" revelation. Typical of the origins of doctrinal statements, the content was conspicuously skewed toward an indirect rebuttal of the "Jesus Name" teaching that was then sweeping through the fledgling movement. The second point of the statement, a fairly straightforward exposition of trinitarian claims, actually contains more words than all the rest of the statement put together.

The advance of Newbigin's trait of orthodoxy—the Protestant tendency to define the church by its beliefs—can be seen among Pentecostals as a result of the post-war relations of the Assemblies of God with Wheaton evangelicalism. This church soon became the largest member church in the National Association of Evangelicals, established in 1942. The embarrassment which led to the defrocking of David du Plessis, described earlier, was at heart a question of orthodoxy: Was this leading Pentecostal church truly "evangelical"?

The same mood, it appears, led to the sole alteration of the Statement of Faith of the Assemblies of God, which occurred in 1961—precisely the year when actions arose resulting in the termination of the ministerial credentials of David du Plessis. With the "Jesus Only" issue prominent and primary in their theological consciousness, the leaders who adopted the 1916 Statement of Fundamental truths had included none of the typical conservative Christological statements about the sinlessness, the deity or even the virgin birth of Christ—highly visible omissions when set against the culture of the new evangelicalism, which preserved the high Christology of their fundamentalist forebears.

The 1961 change introduced a new section on the Deity of Christ. It reads:

3. The Deity of the Lord Jesus Christ

The Lord Jesus Christ is the eternal Son of God. The Scriptures declare:

    (a) His virgin birth (Matthew 1:23; Luke 1:31, 35).

    (b) His sinless life (Hebrews 7:26; 1 Peter 2:22).

    (c) His miracles (Acts 2:22; 10:38).

    (d) His substitutionary work on the cross (1 Corinthians 15:3; 2 Corinthians 5:21).

    (e) His bodily resurrection from the dead (Matthew 28:6; Luke 24:39; 1 Corinthians 15:4).

    (f) His exaltation to the right hand of God (Acts 1:9, 11; 2:33; Philippians 2:9-11; Hebrews 1:3).[9]

Yet the former total of sixteen points in the statement was preserved by merging into one the previously separate points treating the Lord's Supper and water baptism. That the original 1916 Statement contained not sixteen but seventeen points was no part of the collective denominational historical consciousness in 1961—or, for that matter, for years before that.[10]

Still more evidence of creeping orthodoxy in the Assemblies of God emerged with the establishment in 1979 of a Commission on Doctrinal Purity. This body assesses emerging doctrinal emphases that rise easily in a movement where local church sovereignty survives as a strong value. The group reviews possibly deviant teachings expressed by individual ministers of the church and makes recommendations regarding the quality of orthodoxy.

Pentecostal Experience

So although obedience shines through in legalistic and devout Pentecostalism, and orthodoxy grows apace, true religion for Pentecostals is a matter of personal experience. They speak easily of an "experience of God," and they are prone to judge the genuineness of the Christian qualities of others—their "spirituality"—by whether or not there is evidence of personal spiritual experience. Such evidence used to get reported in the testimony meetings that marked earlier Pentecostal services, but which appear to be in decline. Small-group open sharing has become the place where personal spiritual struggles and gains are reported and mutual prayer exchanged.

At times, a person with gifts for public speaking may develop a ministry around a dramatic episode which heightened spiritual experience. Pentecostal evangelist Dave Roevers, for example, has spoken to thousands of American high-schoolers beset with temptations toward substance and sexual abuse. The conspicuous facial scars from a phosphorus grenade that a stray Viet Cong bullet ignited in his hand, have been used effectively by Roevers to stimulate a new sense of patriotism and wholesome personal morality. Dave Roevers speaks from experience, and when he does he speaks as the archetypical Pentecostal minister that he is.

But let a word be said in favor of personal experience. Employers well reward applicants whose level of experience has given them considerable skill. Sick people seek physicians whose wide experience, their practice, has made them specially suited to their illness. Perhaps American pragmatism has elevated the role of personal religious experience among Pentecostals in that nation. But Pentecostals worldwide are those whose personal stories report significant rescues ("salvations") from entrapments of personal habit or from lifestyles of meaningless-ness. What makes the Pentecostal experience of speaking in tongues of particular interest is that it is an intimately personal experience.

Naturally, personal experience can be overplayed. In the social en-vironment of a local congregation, satisfactory levels of personal expe-rience can easily be defined in needlessly narrow ways. Stereotypes evolve. The uninitiated get excluded, and sometimes they wrongly con-fuse congregational rejection with divine disapproval.

At the other end of the scale, emphasis on personal experience can lead to a selfish spiritual narcissism which neglects the needs of others. Or worse, to an elitism that breeds contempt for those whose experi-ence does not match the accepted norm. Such groups thus create for themselves an isolation that does not make them ready participants in joint community or ecclesiastical enterprises.

While such characterizations are surely true of some local Pentecos-tal congregations, they do not adequately describe the movement as a whole. There is an abundance of wise leadership among Pentecostals, particularly in the establishment Pentecostal churches where extensive written corporate guidelines have developed over two generations of dealing with entrepreneurial independent charismatic leaders. At their best, Pentecostals insist on personal religious experience, but they bal-ance individualism with ecclesiastical accountability.

Incidentally, unless the term is unusually defined, it would be wrong to describe the Pentecostal outlook as "mystical experience" in the history-of-religions sense popularized in William James's classic *The Varieties of Religious Experience*. When speaking in tongues, in the re-ligious faint commonly called being "slain in the spirit," Pentecostals do not lose consciousness. They do not seek a vague "nothingness" or the disappearance of the self. Even their occasional reports of visions are rather open-eyed. Pentecostals have no interest in Nirvana. Excep-tions to this general rule would likely emerge among Roman Catholic Pentecostalism, which draws on a lush tradition of mystical experience. References to speaking in tongues among the great Roman Catholic mystics, on the other hand—persons like John of the Cross or Theresa of Avila—are scant.

When the primacy of personal experience for Pentecostals is clear, other features of Pentecostal spirituality make ready sense. These include the high value placed on personal testimony, lively music, common though separate oral prayer that will seem to some noisy and disorderly, deep religious feeling, marked interest in the "presence of God" (which is experienced) and excessive emotionalism where at times distortions of feeling occur or in the throes of initial Pentecostal experience.

Prayer(s)

Only occasionally in the schedule of the typical Pentecostal church is a visitor likely to hear the congregation jointly uttering the same prayer. One is at weddings, where Pentecostals become their most liturgical—often using the traditional Episcopal wedding service that contains written prayers. The other is the Lord's Prayer, always uttered in a common voice, which might be used on special occasions or, increasingly, at ecumenical gatherings. The Lord's Prayer naturally is used more frequently and predictably among the more liturgical charismatic churches—Lutheran, Episcopal, Roman Catholic—where it is a clearly fixed part of the tradition. Pentecostals do not generally show familiarity with the surprisingly plural form "prayers" in a passage otherwise often cited: "and they continued steadfastly in the apostles' doctrine and fellowship, and in breaking of bread, and in prayers" (Acts 2:42 KJV).

For Pentecostals, prayer is talking with God. You can do that alone or joined by other Christians, as few as one other or as many as scores of thousands gathered in charismatic assembly. You can pray in the vernacular or in tongues. It is not uncommon to hear Pentecostals (less likely, charismatics) praying together in tongues all at once, each saying different things. A worship leader might call for such an expression with words like "Let's all pray to God together in our own tongues." In many local churches, the tradition is sufficiently well established to need no pastoral direction. When "Let's pray" is mentioned, all pray for a while at once and in tongues. When the sacred noise subsides this may be followed by a vernacular prayer offered by the pastoral leader who called for prayer, or by someone whom the leader has designated.

In the 1930s and 1940s, American classical Pentecostals were inclined to kneel in prayer. Today they more commonly stand. Then and now in collective or private prayer, they are wont to raise their hands, palms forward and fingers spread, as a posture of prayer. There is more truth than fiction in distinction, often humorously made, between Pentecostals who raise arms fully overhead, palms forward, and charismatics who extend arms palms up, elbows at the waist.

There is a third situation where Pentecostals join in common vernacular prayer (but not only they, other evangelicals do the same). This occurs when the evangelist or pastor asks the congregation to repeat after him a prayer, sentence by sentence—an ad hoc prayer spontaneously composed. This is usually done to help someone brand new to the faith to say an entry prayer.

In private prayer, Pentecostals make use of speaking in tongues, their "private prayer language." Often quoted as justification is 1 Corinthians 14:15: "I will pray with my spirit, but I will also pray with my mind." As do some front-rank New Testament interpreters, Pentecostals take it that glossolalic prayer is described in the familiar words of Romans 8:26: "We do not know what we ought to pray for, but the Spirit himself intercedes for us with groans that words cannot express."

Even in those Pentecostal churches where speaking in tongues as a feature of a public service is rare, many of those gathered will have established habits of personal glossolalic prayer. In such private use, no interpretation is sought or expected, normally. Neither is any interpretation expected in glossolalic group prayer, though biblical warrant for such collective prayer using uninterpreted glossalalia is difficult to provide. Collective glossolalic prayer, it seems, is considerably less frequent among denominational charismatics, though it is nearly a regular feature of most varieties of classical Pentecostalism.

Those who hear Pentecostals pray will often note their enthusiasm and directness. But they also may be offended by the volume and apparent lugubriousness involved. Often there are new Christians from blue-collar sectors of society or the underprivileged for whom, frankly, life has been rough. Little wonder that they pray the same way they do anything else—with vigor and feeling. Remember the priority of experience for Pentecostals.

Charismatics by example have taught Pentecostals that spirituality (in the Pentecostal sense) need not be measured in decibels and that

God is not deaf. The affected, often mournful, holy accent is heard far less among charismatics than it is among Pentecostals. A traditional Pentecostal prayer often presents an appearance of pained obsequiousness. But an opposite feature also appears. Pentecostals are taught holy boldness by the example of their leaders, and in prayer they will often command God (for healing) or Satan (for excision of evil influences).

Before the rise of Pentecostal televangelism, the prayer of lay persons matched the efficacy of those made by clergy. Since then, dominant twice-charismatic personalities who become charismatic celebrities quite often drown out the cries of the little people.

What distinguishes the spirituality of Pentecostals with regard to prayer lies in their ready use of glossalic prayer in public or private, their conspicuous enthusiasm and their characteristic pained expressions. But through it all, heartfelt personal experience predominates.

Holy Laughter

The concept of holy laughter will strike many readers as odd, as well as many contemporary Pentecostals who themselves have never witnessed this phenomenon. Pentecostals from the older, classical era (through the 1950s) knew of an unplanned, unsought, occasional work of the Holy Spirit that was manifest in fits of laughter. The episode might follow speaking in tongues, but far more often, the laughter came on its own.

Normally, such a manifestation began at an altar service—a period of prayer, with believers gathered at the front of the church, invariably kneeling. The pastor, or lay elder might go from one person to another offering whatever spiritual aid seemed proper. I suppose that only those whose lives include this experience can appreciate the spiritual therapy of this sacred laughter, a kind of compacted joy.

There was no sense that such an episode should or even could be repeated: laughter was not an invented charisma, nor was it something anyone should purposely seek. Spontaneity again. Bible-reading Pentecostals had read in their King James Versions about Bildad's counsel to Job: "Behold, God will not cast away a perfect man, neither will he help the evildoers: Till he fill thy mouth with laughing" (Job 8:20-21). They could readily reach for the promise of Jesus, "Blessed are ye that weep now: for ye shall laugh" (Lk 6:21).

For fifteen or twenty minutes, or for an hour or two (Pentecostal altar services could last into the wee hours), the believer who was so moved might laugh. One or two or a few others might join, but it was usually a solo affair. Sympathetic fellow worshipers would smile and offer their own vocal praise to God. The environment rippled with an awesome shared awareness of the experienced presence of God.

Pandemonism

Another feature widely found in Pentecostal spirituality—I'm down to the miscellanies—is what can be termed pandemonism. This is the result of an intensification of belief in evil demons or spirits. In this outlook, deviant or undesirable behaviors are attributed to demons. Involved are not only unwelcome attitudes like sloth or lust, habits like smoking or drinking, pessimism and the like, but even more common human moods like discouragement, sadness, mourning—whatever is perceived as less than a full-scaled ebullience of joy, peace and love.

If such states are caused by spirits, the cure must be their expulsion. Hence there flourishes among Pentecostals a "ministry of deliverance," which is not at all limited to charismatic leadership but can be practiced by sympathetic laity as well.

Probably due to the impact of charismatic television programming, Pentecostals have easily absorbed this widespread demonism and have come to regard exorcism as one of the more powerful spiritual gifts—even though the word *demon* does not appear in the King James Version (which regularly uses the word *devil* instead), nor is exorcism ever expressly described as a charismatic gift in Scripture.

It is true to say that pandemonism flourishes more among independent and electronic Pentecostals. The more established Pentecostal bodies do not encourage a dour Christian life, and one church—the Assemblies of God—has published a position paper flatly denying that Christians can be possessed by demons.

It is worth recalling on this subject the words of Swiss theologian Karl Barth. He likened giving attention to demons to viewing an active but quiescent volcano: a single, brief, "momentary glance" is enough.[11]

A Pentecostal Lexicon

The spirituality of a people appears in their language, and Pentecostals are not without their own sacred jargon. Here is a brief dictionary of terms, many of which never make it into respectable theological prose, but all of which mark the oral culture of Pentecostalism and reflect its spirituality.

The presence of God refers to the collective sense of the gathered Christians that God is unusually present in a meeting. Outsiders will think it strange that an extraordinary instance of the perceived presence of God might be reported this way: "God was so powerfully present that the pastor did not give his sermon today." It is not that Pentecostals do not value the Word of God; they rather give way, on occasion, to collective and extended oral praise of God. This means a prayerful environment, perhaps prophecies and messages in tongues, with interpretations to follow.

Another way to describe such an event, in Pentecostal parlance, is to say that *the power of the Lord came down*. Here again the collective, corporate religious experience is valued.

Slain in the Spirit has been retitled by charismatics as *resting in the Spirit* or *falling in the Spirit*. There are moments (sometimes hours) in Pentecostal services where a believer falls to the floor in a religious faint. Some Pentecostals call this being *slain under the power*. The charismatic retitling was motivated by a desire to avoid militaristic language (*slain*).

Such events in their genuine forms occur spontaneously. Over the past couple of decades, enthusiastic platform leaders developed the practice of laying hands on the person, usually on the forehead. To many observers, the subject seems nearly to be pushed over. In contrast, early Pentecostal episodes of this *slaying in the Spirit* uniformly happened with no one nearby aiding the process. This phenomenon deserves considerably more study than it has received.

Filled with the baptism is really a conflation of *filled with the Spirit* and *baptized in the Spirit*. One of the sociological hazards of Pentecostalism appears in its potential to overemphasize experience. Hence the emphasis shifts from the Spirit to what the Spirit does—baptism. All too easily, Pentecostal devotees can, in the charged environment of an enthusiastic service probably managed by a conspicuous leader, find their attention shifted from the Spirit to the experience of the Spirit. A worthy goal for Pentecostals, widely achieved but often threatened, is the balanced mix of Word and Spirit.

Prayer language is a recent (maybe since 1965) synonym for glossolalia. There is no uniform understanding among Pentecostals as to whether the tongue in which they speak is one of the existing world languages. If not, they are not at all troubled since there are tongues of angels and since no one understands the speaker of tongues (1 Cor 14:2). The term *prayer language,* which is probably of charismatic rather than Pentecostal origin, implies what is not always true among Pentecostals—that the initial evidence of glossolalia stays on as a residual and blessed ability. Pentecostal doctrine, in fact, does not require that the devotee speak in tongues ever again (though many do) following the baptism of the Spirit.

Word of knowledge takes on a particular meaning among Pentecostals and charismatics—one, it is worth noting, which is allowed but not required by the exact biblical wording at 1 Corinthians 12:8, the sole place in Scripture where the gift is mentioned (though in Pentecostal understanding, examples can be found elsewhere). Typically a platform leader will announce that a person present has a physical ailment which, if admitted, may be healed through prayer which is then offered. Other personal matters may be declared in addition to illnesses. These are understood to be divine disclosures given to the leader, and some leaders test credibility by structuring the service so that they alone receive such *words.* More balanced Pentecostal teaching allows that any believer may receive such a *word.* In fact, however, few do.

Evaluating Pentecostal Spirituality

The excesses and inadequacies of Pentecostal spirituality may be more apparent than its undoubted interior realities. Certainly, both weaknesses and strengths emerge.

The emphasis on personal experience has the advantage of creating individually crafted Christians. But it leads also to an ever-present temptation toward elitism—an unwarranted celebration of presumed spiritual superiority. While it does a lot for personal spiritual growth to open up to charismatic potentials in one's life and ministry, the surest measure of a pilgrim's progress will always be faith, hope and love. *Never* will it be the spectacular performance of charismatic endowments.

What more sobering word of Scripture can there be for Pentecostals and charismatics, tempted to value the gift above the Giver, than those startling words of Jesus spoken to effective (but defective) charismatics who pled the efficacy of their prophecies and their exorcisms before Jesus? His sobering response: "Then I will tell them plainly, 'I never knew you. Away from me, you evildoers!' " (Mt 7:23). Charisma must never be divorced from character.

The occupational hazards of Pentecostalism are clear: the opportunity for triumphalism, unloving elitism, distorted interest in charismatic peculiarities, ahistorical social insensitivity, theological impoverishment—and there are more. Yet for all its imperfections, today's dominant breed of Protestantism, which has already spilled over to all other sectors of the church, offers a simple enrichment to personal faith—the capacity to pray in the Spirit and to pray with the mind also. Why fault them if, in this way, they love God and enjoy him forever?

Notes

[1]David B. Barrett, *World Christian Encyclopedia: A Comparative Study of Churches and Religions in the Modern World*, A.D. *1900-2000* (New York: Oxford University Press, 1982). An important review by Stephan Neill, who served as a consultant to the *Encyclopedia*, appears in *Missiology: An International Review* 12 (January 1984), pp. 5-19. Figures in the first paragraph come from Barrett's annual update published as "Annual Statistical Table on Global Mission: 1987," *International Bulletin of Missionary Research* 12 (January 1987), pp. 24-25.

[2]Personal communication with David Barrett on December 4, 1987.

[3]The intricate theological movements from Wesleyan roots have been traced competently by Donald W. Dayton, *Theological Roots of Pentecostalism* (Metuchen, N.J.: Scarecrow Press; and Grand Rapids, Mich.: Zondervan; both 1987), a reworking of an earlier University of Chicago Ph.D. dissertation.

[4]*New Covenant*, a leading charismatic periodical established in 1971, despite clear-cut Roman Catholic origins, reflected the broad contours of the charismatic movement in its issues published during the 1970s. But through the middle 1980s the magazine increasingly has returned to a decidedly Roman Catholic orientation. Although the narrowed thrust may be viewed by some as counterproductive, in fact the effect is to consolidate, domesticate and integrate charismatic spirituality into the largest of Christian churches and thus to reduce its potential for divisiveness.

[5]Jon Alexander treats mainly Roman Catholic writers when he asked "What Do Recent Writers Mean by Spirituality?" *Spirituality Today* 32 (1981), pp. 247-56. But this limitation shows indirectly that the Roman Catholic tradition is the primary source of the popularity of the term today.

[6]Lesslie Newbigin, *The Household of God: Lectures on the Nature of the Church* (New York: Friendship Press, 1954).

[7]"Orthodoxy," "obedient participation" (and later, "obedience") and "experience" are

my terms—not Newbigin's.

[8]*Combined Minutes of the General Council of the Assemblies of God, April 2-12, November 15-29, 1914* (St. Louis, Mo.: Gospel Publishing House, 1915), p. 4.

[9]Constitution and Bylaws, Article 5, Section 3 in *Minutes of the 41st Session of the General Council of the Assemblies of God, August 8-13, 1985* (Springfield, Mo.: Gospel Publishing House, 1985), p. 106.

[10]Actually there were seventeen points in the original 1916 "Statement of Fundamental Truths." Point 13 of "The Essentials of the Godhead" eventually was merged into point 2, "The One True God," where it has remained. From at least 1922 onward, the Statement itemized sixteen points.

[11]My colleague Cecil M. Robeck, Jr., showed me the reference in Barth *(Church Dogmatics* 3.3.51, p. 519) and observed that Barth, who had just devoted 152 pages in his systematic theology to angels, would give but twelve pages to demons.

The Lutheran Response
Gerhard. O. Forde

FIRST LET ME SAY THAT I AM GRATEFUL FOR DR. SPITTLER'S CARE-
ful, critical and enlightening presentation of Pentecostal views
on spirituality. It is a very helpful treatment.

I would like to respond to the major question that Spittler raises at
the end. Since this is "today's dominant breed" of Protestantism and
it has spilled over into even Roman Catholic and Eastern Orthodox
Christianity and since it offers a simple enrichment to personal faith,
why fault it if in this way its practitioners are encouraged to love God
and enjoy him forever? A more or less pragmatic argument. If it works
for some, indeed many, and doesn't seem to do any obvious harm, why
argue with it?

Aside from the fact that it is just the job of theologians to argue
about theological positions and their grounding, however pragmatical-
ly successful they may be, it is necessary in this case particularly to try
to get a theological fix on just what Pentecostalism and the charismatic
movement represent. That is, in order to answer Spittler's question we
need some way to assess the movement and its spirituality theologically.
One cannot simply overlook the fact that the movement has encoun-
tered considerable opposition from all quarters of the church and continues to do so. What is the root of this opposition and suspicion? That
seems the place to start, and I do not believe that it has been very clearly

spelled out heretofore.

Now this is hardly the place to attempt an exhaustive theological analysis, and so what follows shall have to be taken as sketchy and perhaps even overdrawn at times. In a nutshell, Pentecostal and charismatic spirituality represents the culmination of the problem I have been talking about: the problem of the difference between *talking about* sanctification or spirituality, however correctly, and speaking in a way that will actually bring sanctification. This is the crux of the problem of speaking law and gospel. As such it points up the failure to speak the gospel and so is a manifestation of the bad conscience of Protestantism. The fact that it is the dominant breed of Protestantism today is not encouraging in this light.

The challenge is speaking a gospel which actually puts an end to the law and brings about gospel living. When people are constantly confronted with talk about how they must become holy, how they must have the Spirit to become so, how they must show their sanctification now that they have been justified—it is no wonder that peculiar things begin to happen! The law never really ends. No matter how correct the talk of sanctification may be theologically, the gospel has been eclipsed and people fall under the law once again. Is it, therefore, mere coincidence that Pentecostalism grows out of holiness sects?

Since these movements lay claim to the Spirit and various experiences thereof, it is ultimately the theological interpretation of the Spirit that is at stake. Again, this is not the place to tackle that problem in any depth. Suffice it to say that the problem throughout the tradition has been with various kinds of divorce between Word and Spirit. Spirit did not come *through* the Word, but was to be sought beyond or above it somehow. In the early and middle ages this was to be accomplished through spiritual exegesis, perhaps, and reified in mystical experience. The Reformation, particularly in Luther's hermeneutical development, insisted that the Spirit comes through the Word as the gospel's enlivening and liberating voice. This occurs when the letter (the law) puts the old being to death and raises up the new in the Spirit.

"The letter kills, but the Spirit gives life." That is, the Spirit is precisely unleashed upon us in the properly preached gospel, the Word of the crucified and risen one, which sets us free. It simply is not, in this view, a "free-floating" and occasional "force" which may or may not visit this person or that one. All such "free-floating" spirits detached from the gospel were highly suspect and deemed likely only to bind to the law in one subtle way or another. The Spirit is detached from the Trinity. So Luther, in outspoken fashion, could simply declare in the Smalcald Articles that "whatever is attributed to the Spirit apart from the Word and the sacraments is of the devil." Why the devil? Because the devil too is spirit, of course, but he is also the enemy, the accuser, the spirit of slavery.

Now the post-Reformation world did not generally understand or appreciate this critique of spiritualism. The result has been an even more drastic split between Word and Spirit. Rejecting the medieval spiritual exegesis and failing to understand the Reformation's association of gospel-Word and Spirit, modern Protestantism landed simply in the prison of literalism with all its problems. The Word of God, which as gospel is Spirit and life, degenerated into words *about* God and Jesus which tend to be mere information.

Those literalists who want to insist on the inerrancy of this information are generally reluctant to credit extraneous and independent manifestations of Spirit—thus the opposition between fundamentalists and charismatics. But the literalist interpretation just does not allow for an experience of the Spirit in "the letter," even though there is constant talk *about* the Spirit. Since there is no Spirit in or with the letter, he is to be sought, expected or cultivated elsewhere. *Spirit* becomes a transcendent, occasional, arbitrary force, a secret agenda. If such Spirit is to be routinized, one can only pay careful attention to how those who profess to have gotten it managed to do so, and attempt in some fashion to imitate them. And so we find ourselves once again under the law. Perhaps Pentecostalism's own embarrassment at this result is manifest in the ongoing uncertainty and debate about just what experiences of Spirit describe true faith.

So Spittler's question would have to be answered, I think, from the perspective of a theological understanding of the Spirit. No doubt Pentecostals and charismatics have done many good things. But what is at stake is always the gospel. Spirit detached from the preached Word of the gospel and the sacraments can be devastating. There is, after all, more than one spirit; and we are admonished to test them lest we fall prey to the wrong ones.

A Reformed Response
Sinclair B. Ferguson

PROFESSOR SPITTLER HAS PROVIDED A HIGHLY INFORMATIVE ES-
say covering a wide range of issues in the multifaceted world
of Pentecostal and charismatic thinking. The face of the Christian church has been powerfully influenced by such thinking. There can
be little doubt that it has stirred older groupings of Christians into
asking serious questions about what it means to be the body of Christ
in a vital, Spirit-empowered way.

The contrast between Reformed theology and Pentecostal-charismatic theology is very considerable in places. Perhaps the best brief response to Dr. Spittler's overview therefore is simply to outline a
number of problems Reformed theology generally has with classic Pentecostal-charismatic theology.

The first problem is that Reformed theology sees the day of Pentecost and its accompaniments as a unique, unrepeatable event. It belongs, in technical language, to the *historia salutis* (history of redemption), not to the *ordo salutis* (order of the application of redemption to
the individual).

Scripture does not encourage us to have our own personal Pentecost
(or our personal Calvary). These are once-for-all events in history.
Their consequences become ours immediately, but progressively, when

we are united to Christ crucified, buried, raised, seated at God's right hand and destined to return in glory (Rom 6:1-10; Gal 2:20; Eph 2:4-7; Col 2:9-15; 3:1-4). But the events themselves are never repeated or repeatable.

Second, Reformed theology sees Pentecost as a Christological and Christocentric event. It is the earthly manifestation of the heavenly coronation of Jesus Christ as Messiah-King. (Hence, *in the nature of the case,* the lavish outpouring of gifts at Pentecost was never expected to be a permanent phenomenon—a point less readily understood in a democracy than in a monarchy!). Both our Lord Jesus Christ and Simon Peter interpreted Pentecost Christocentrically (compare Jn 16:7-11, a specific prophecy of Pentecost; Acts 2:22-36, Peter's explanation of the Spirit's coming lies in what he says about Christ).

For this reason, Reformed theology, while recognizing that the Christian may experience the Spirit's ministry in many different ways, refuses to formalize such experiences in a theology of subsequence. These further experiences are simply richer and fuller manifestations of Christ and his riches to the Christian (compare the promise of this in an *uncategorized fashion* in John 14:16-21).

Third, Reformed theology has generally held that, while God continues to do mighty works in his world, not least in answer to prayer, certain *gifts* given to the church were intended for use only as an interim measure. If asked, for example, how it is possible to deny that the worldwide twentieth-century phenomenon of tongues-speaking, for example, is an outpouring of the Spirit, the answer (however unacceptable to charismatics) is that speaking in tongues is a physical phenomenon that can be voluntarily learned and exhibited (the tongues I have heard from committed noncharismatics were indistinguishable from those uttered by charismatics). Tongues are not a necessary sign of the work of the Spirit. Consequently the frequency of the phenomenon does not of itself indicate that it is a fruit of the Spirit's ministry. The same can be said of other gifts. In light of the numerical strength of the charismatic movement (well underscored by Dr. Spittler), it has become commonplace to treat this older Reformed position as reactionary, unsophisticated, anti-experimental and dogmatic.

Space permits only the briefest indication of the salient points of the Reformed argument that certain gifts decreased in exercise as the apostolic age drew to a close and the canon of Scripture was increasingly recognized.

First, the gift of working miraculous signs was not "commonplace" in the New Testament church. They had a specific confirmatory function in connection with the apostolic proclamation of the New Covenant (Acts 2:2; 14:3; 2 Cor 3:6), just as the ministries of Moses, Elijah, Elisha and Daniel were confirmed by signs and wonders in times of critical importance for God's Old-Covenant people. In fact, there is a great economy of signs and wonders in Scripture. The biblical pattern as a whole is that such works and gifts are neither normal nor normative for the people of God.

Consequently, certain gifts were defined in the New Testament as "the thing that mark an apostle—signs, wonders and miracles" (2 Cor 12:12; compare to Acts 15:12; Heb 2:1-4). In fact, there is no record that these gifts were distributed to the church in the widespread fashion sometimes alleged. (Stephen and Philip, who clearly operated under apostolic authority and guidelines, are the only persons named as workers of miracles outside the apostolic group.) It is highly significant that there is no indication in the apostolic vision for the future church (in 1 and 2 Timothy and Titus) that these gifts would continue to play a role. Instead we find a self-conscious stress on the complete adequacy of Scripture (2 Tim 3:15-17).

Second, the gifts of prophecy and interpreted tongues used as vehicles of divine revelation had a built-in impermanence. They were the Urim and Thummin of the infant church. But their permanence was no more guaranteed than that of those guiding stones used in the Old Testament to discern God's will. Now the church turns to Scripture alone to answer the question: "What is God's revealed will?"

This does not deny the vital role of spiritual discernment. Feelings, senses, hunches and convictions may well be the fruit of God's Word working in our hearts, even at a subconscious level. But they should never be prefaced by "this is what the Sovereign Lord says."

Third, Reformed theology has no quarrel with an emphasis on experience. Rather, its concern is the fascination of many Pentecostal-charismatics with the immediate (God speaking directly, today, through a medium other than Scripture). Furthermore, Reformed Christians are troubled to see their brothers and sisters intrigued by the *abnormal* (tongues, prophecies, holy laughter, slaying in the Spirit, exorcism of the demons of the flu, depression, lying and so on).

The question raised here is: Does not the claim to have immediate access to the will of God revealed elsewhere than in his mediated revelation in Scripture downplay the authoritative role of Scripture and its sufficiency, no matter what doctrine of Scripture is publicly espoused? At stake here is the Reformation principle of *sola Scriptura*—Scripture as our sole authority. On this issue particularly it is inevitable that Reformed theology should act as the church's conscience and be concerned to safeguard God's Word.

A Wesleyan Response
Laurence W. Wood

DR. *SPITTLER CORRECTLY POINTS OUT THAT "THE ACCEP-*
tance of speaking in tongues as a legitimate, and even necessary, variety of Christian experience" is the decisive difference between the Pentecostal and the Wesleyan-holiness traditions.
With this one difference, the Pentecostals were Wesleyan in their view
of sanctification. I would like to point out that this Wesleyan element
is almost lacking entirely in Spittler's essay. Furthermore, the Pentecostal emphasis on the in-filling of the Spirit is an explicit aspect of
original Methodism and is not introduced as a later imposition by the
nineteenth-century American Wesleyan-holiness tradition.

While the Wesleyan-holiness tradition taught that believers should
receive the baptism in the Holy Spirit, Spittler points out that it was
the Pentecostal groups who first began the movement of tongues-
speaking as "the initial physical evidence" of this experience. Spittler
says it was not until the last quarter of the nineteenth century that the
holiness group began emphasizing the baptism in the Holy Spirit;
however, this is inaccurate since the emphasis on the baptism or in-
filling of the Holy Spirit dates back to John Fletcher, Wesley's closest
friend and the "second founder" of the Methodist movement. In my
book *Pentecostal Grace* I have pointed out that Fletcher equated Wesley's

doctrine of perfect love with the Pentecostal in-filling of the Spirit. This emphasis was not a further development within the Wesleyan-holiness tradition, but was a conspicuous part of the very beginning of the Wesleyan movement.

Though Wesley insisted that all believers "received the Spirit" in conversion, he also equated perfect love with being filled with the Spirit on occasions, including at least one reference in his *Plain Account of Christian Perfection* (p. 55). This equation of the Pentecostal in-filling of the Holy Spirit with the perfection of love was, however, Fletcher's favorite expression, as Wesley noted in his biography of Fletcher. Though this was not Wesley's usual term for sanctification, his emphasis on the fruit of the Spirit as being the essence of the sanctified life, along with his trinitarian interpretation of the different stages of Christian experience, implicitly brings him into agreement with Fletcher on this point. It is also significant that Wesley assumed responsibility for publishing Fletcher's writings. Fletcher had given Wesley complete freedom to edit his theology. Wesley's response to Fletcher was that there was no real disagreement between them in their theology. Interestingly enough, Fletcher insists throughout his writings that there was no substantial disagreement between himself and Wesley, yet he acknowledged that there was a verbal difference between them in their manner of expression. Fletcher says that Wesley uses the language of the "rational divine" and speaks of sanctification largely in theological-logical terms, while Fletcher uses the biblical phrase of "baptism in the Holy Spirit." Fletcher further defends this equation by referring to their Anglican theology of confirmation which was a liturgical-sacramental rite signifying that the believer who had already been baptized with water at infancy was in this new event of confirmation being baptized with the Holy Spirit. Actually, the Wesleyan doctrine of two works of grace was an "evangelicalizing" of the Anglican sacraments of baptism and confirmation, as I have pointed out in *Pentecostal Grace*.

The nineteenth-century Wesleyan-holiness tradition was not at all departing from its Wesleyan roots by emphasizing the Spirit-filled life. Melvin Dieter writes: "The adoption of Pentecostal and Baptism of the Holy Ghost paradigms as the major vehicle for the expression of Holiness thought and preaching by the close of the [nineteenth] century was no introduction of an unnatural or unWesleyan element into the holiness tradition; rather, it was a natural outgrowth of a weighted factor in Wesley's own teaching on Christian Perfection and the work and witness of the Holy Spirit in persons and in the world which demanded theological explication" [*The Wesleyan Theological Journal* 20, no. 1 (Spring 1985), p. 67]. However, the camp-meeting revivalist experience was a radicalizing of its Wesleyan roots in the sense that the sacramental understanding of the church was largely dropped in favor of the subjectivist-individualistic experience.

The Pentecostal movement was a further radicalizing of this individualistic notion of Christian experience with the new development of tongues-speaking. Not only was the rise of tongues-speaking something new, but the idea that it was the necessary physical evidence of being filled with the Spirit was a novel interpretation as well. On the other hand, the Pentecostal movement was Wesleyan in its beginnings.

The Wesleyan-holiness tradition thus has much in common with Pentecostalism, especially with the emphasis on the personal awareness of the presence of God through the in-filling of the Holy Spirit. Wesley referred to this personal dimension as "experimental religion." This meant for Wesley that the believer can have a personal experience with Christ which is accompanied by the inner testimony of the Holy Spirit.

It is thus understandable that Pentecostalism first arose from within the Wesleyan-holiness tradition. For its emphasis on tongues-speaking as evidence of Christian experience is an extension of the Wesleyan doctrine of the inner assurance of faith. For Wesley, however, the inner witness did not mean a highly charged emotional or physical sign. Rather, the evidence of God in the heart of the believer was a calm assurance that he or she is accepted by God. Wesley disliked emotionalism. Worship was to be done "in a fitting and orderly way" (1 Cor 14:40). But the Wesleyan-holiness tradition in the nineteenth century in America accentuated Wesley's teaching on the witness of the Spirit to such a degree that emotional displays such as shouting came to be accepted as the outward evidence of the work of the Spirit.

It was out of this kind of Wesleyan-holiness background that the Pentecostal groups were begun with tongues-speaking as the distinctive evidence of spirituality. This new development provoked immediate negative reaction within the Wesleyan-holiness groups who were quick to disassociate themselves from their Pentecostal offshoots in the early part of the twentieth century. The Wesleyan-holiness churches quickly dropped the word "Pentecostal" from their official vocabulary so that they would not be associated with the newly emerging Pentecostal churches.

To elevate the gift of tongues as the prized possession of Christian experience seemed to be contrary to Paul's listing tongues-speaking as the least of the gifts (in 1 Cor 12:27-31). In 1 Corinthians 14, Paul seemed to be making a fairly negative statement about whatever the Corinthians were doing in the way of tongues-speaking. To take something out of its negative context and make it the test of Christian experience seemed bad exegesis. Further, Wesleyan-holiness writers pointed out that in other places where the gifts of the Spirit were listed, the gift of tongues and interpretation of tongues were completely omitted (Eph 4:11; Rom 12:6-8), which would seem to be difficult to explain if tongues-speaking were so decisive a test of spirituality.

Now that the Pentecostal movement has become less insistent in many instances on tongues-speaking as the necessary evidence of spirituality, and with the rise of the broader charismatic renewal groups in mainline denominations, many in the Wesleyan-holiness traditions are less suspicious and more friendly toward Pentecostals and charismatics.

Because of the more moderate stance of the Pentecostal groups in their further developed tradition, and because of the emphasis on vital piety in the charismatic renewal movements, many in the Wesleyan-holiness tradition are now friendly toward, and cooperative with, the efforts and goals of a deeper spirituality encouraged by the Pentecostal and charismatic movements. Many in the Wesleyan-holiness tradition feel that a renewed emphasis on the gifts of the Spirit could provide a theological basis for building a stronger sense of Christian community and deeper understanding of the meaning of the church as the body of Christ. To this extent, the Wesleyan-holiness tradition is indebted to the Pentecostal-charismatic movement.

Wesleyan theological distinctives are certainly compatible with the spiritual vitality of the Pentecostal-charismatic groups. However, the Wesleyan movements would like to see the Pentecostal-charismatic groups incorporate more of a Wesleyan emphasis on *purity of heart* (sanctification) as the essential meaning of Pentecostal spirituality. At the same time, it should be said that many in the Wesleyan-holiness tradition appreciate the way that the Pentecostal-charismatic movements have emphasized the importance of the Spirit-filled life. Without this dynamic of the Pentecostal outpouring of the Spirit in the life of the believer, the Wesleyan doctrine of sanctification could easily degenerate into a lifeless, formal concept of ethics.

It is my personal hope that a blend of Pentecostal-charismatic Christianity with its emphasis on the gifts of the Spirit and the Wesleyan-holiness tradition with its emphasis on the fruit of the Spirit might be synthesized into a larger understanding of the meaning of Pentecostal reality. In order for this synthesis to occur, the following issues need to be addressed in a spirit of collegiality and amicable dialog between the Wesleyan-holiness tradition and the Pentecostal-charismatic movements:

First, the Anglo-Catholic sacraments of baptism and confirmation as the background for understanding the basis for the two distinct events of conversion-initiation and the Spirit-filled life. This theme would lead to a further investigation of the relevance of the sacraments for Christian experience, as well as to a reexamination of the corporate nature of the church.

Second, the relationship between the fruit of the Spirit (sanctification) and the gifts of the Spirit (edification). This discussion would focus on these two aspects of the broader meaning of the baptism with the Holy Spirit.

Third, the relationship between the gift of the Spirit and the gifts of the Spirit. This theme would examine especially the necessity of all believers being recipients of the Spirit, with an appreciation for the different gifts of the Spirit distributed to believers by divine sovereignty.

Fourth, the relationship between the gifts of the Spirit and the outward evidence of the Spirit's work in the believing community. This theme would explore the doctrine of the inner assurance of faith and the kinds of evidences a believer should have as being characteristic of his or her life in Christ.

Fifth, the relationship between the intellectual and emotional components of religious experience. This theme would especially explore the role of experience as a basis for formulating a theology. To what

extent is the believer's experience the necessary basis for a right interpretation of the biblical revelation?

Sixth, the role of tongues-speaking as a valid or necessary gift for the
experience of the church in today's world. This theme would perhaps
be the most troublesome part of such a dialog between the Wesleyan
and the Pentecostal groups, though it would be less controversial for
the broader charismatic renewal groups. Yet neither the Wesleyan-holiness tradition nor the Pentecostal-charismatic groups should want to
avoid such a discussion if our witness in today's world is to be max-
imally effective. I believe our different but similar traditions would
profit greatly by such an ongoing dialog.

Whatever differences might exist between the Wesleyan-holiness tradition and the Pentecostal groups, I personally commend my Pentecostal brothers and sisters in Christ for their powerful witness to the
reality of our risen Lord in the contemporary world. I am especially
appreciative of their emphasis on the need for believers to experience
their own personal Pentecost. For I believe God raised up the Pentecostal denominations and the charismatic renewal groups for the specific purpose of witnessing to the contemporary relevance of believers
coming into an experience of the Spirit's fullness. Pentecost was not
merely a historical event of the past; contemporary disciples of Christ
need to "tarry in the upper room" until they too are endued with the
purifying power of the Holy Spirit! Certainly this is the essence of the
sanctified life. In an age of pretentious intellectualism and shallow
emotionalism, the scriptural call for believers to be filled with the Holy
Spirit is indeed God's Word for today.

A Contemplative Response
E. Glenn Hinson

THIS IS AN EXCELLENT INTRODUCTION TO PENTECOSTAL SPIRI-
tuality, although it says little about spiritual growth and development, or sanctification. Is that a consequence of the
general nature of Dr. Spittler's article, or is it due to the fact that
Pentecostalism values this concept less than it does other elements of
spirituality? One would think that the Wesleyan form of Pentecostalism, the oldest form, would place quite a premium on sanctification,
but no special attention has been given to that in the article.

This is not to say that Pentecostal spirituality has little in common
with the contemplative tradition. Both accentuate experience. Both
look on obedience to God as the central concern. Both tiptoe gingerly
down the path of "orthodoxy," sometimes challenging cut-and-dried
formulas. Both emphasize personal experience more than theological
precision. Both view prayer as a Christian's central occupation. Both
show a healthy respect for the power of the demonic and perhaps
engage in the same "holy laughter." Both pay heed to the Holy Spirit's
role in Christian life and thought. So the commonalties are extensive,
and it would probably be safe to say that many contemplatives would
have felt comfortable in Pentecostal settings as they do today in charismatic contexts.

Yet one cannot read this essay without realizing that contemplatives and Pentecostals walk quite different paths. Contemplatives are concerned with the radical transformation of persons through a gradual process requiring, more often than not, a step-by-step surrender and abandonment to God. Pentecostals, on the other hand, usually expect some kind of instantaneous change connected with speaking in tongues. Neo-Pentecostals or charismatics may not look upon the latter as "a matter of necessity," but Pentecostals do. For them, moreover, spirituality focuses far more on such experiences than it does on growth in grace and the knowledge of God. The great spiritual masters regularly warn against over-reliance on experience as a barometer of sanctity. Experiences may mislead. Too much lusting after experience may plunge one into a religious swamp from which it would be difficult to extract oneself. A healthy spirituality, as Baron Friedrich von Hugel pointed out years ago, balances the experiential with intellectual, social and institutional dimensions.

This is precisely where the "catholic" tradition would fault the Pentecostal tradition of spirituality. In excessive zeal for experience, Pentecostalism has often neglected the intellectual, lapsing at times not only into an indifference about theology but also into an anti-intellectualism. Hostility to "faith seeking understanding" may well explain the creeping creedalism in the Assemblies of God.

Pentecostalism has likewise shortchanged social service and action. Admittedly, slighting of these would be characteristic of persons of lower socioeconomic and cultural backgrounds who make up the Pentecostal constituency, and Pentecostals do render a social service within such a constituency. But it is revealing that Dr. Spittler nowhere mentions social concern as an aspect of spirituality, for this signifies that, as a Pentecostal, he does not link it directly to spirituality.

Finally, Pentecostals have sometimes looked askance at institutional expressions of Christianity. Although Dr. Spittler names some prayer forms or confessions used in Pentecostal churches, most observers are conscious of the strain on orderliness in worship and in church structures that Pentecostals often create. The Spirit must be allowed to blow as the Spirit wills.

Pentecostals and charismatics deserve commendation for their emphasis on the Holy Spirit and for injecting new life into other churches.

The charismatic-Pentecostal movement represents one of the fastest growing and most vital expressions of Christianity not only in the United States but in secular Europe, Africa and Latin America. Such growth would not have occurred had this tradition not had something to offer. In all of these areas, however, Pentecostalism has endangered itself and its mission by an imbalance on the experiential side. Some of the other elements may intrude in and of themselves, but balance will be difficult to attain without the reworking of Pentecostal theology in the way charismatics in the Roman Catholic Church have had to do. Revision should probably start with renewed emphasis on the incarnate Word and wisdom of God. Such an emphasis would surely shift some of the concern of Pentecostals to intellectual, social and institutional spheres badly neglected by most of its representatives.

The Contemplative View
E. Glenn Hinson

THOMAS KELLY HAS REMINDED US THAT WE MAY ALL LIVE LIFE on two levels. One is the level of activities. Some people live life only on this level. They run breathlessly and frantically through crowded calendars of appointments, caught up in activities for activities' sake. No voice speaks from the depths to challenge and inform what they are doing.

But there is another level on which we may live life. That is the level of the interior life—where we commune, communicate, converse with God. When we first become serious about our relationship with God, Kelly says, we may alternate between these two levels. Now we engage in activities; now in communion, communication, conversation with God. But as we grow and develop in our relationship with God, we may do these simultaneously. Not now one and now the other, but rather while we engage in our activities, at the same time, quietly behind the scenes, we carry on our secret communion. In this way our relationship with God transfuses and informs everything we are doing.[1]

Seventeenth-century Carmelite Brother Lawrence wrote of "the practice of the presence of God." While cooking and washing dishes in the monastery kitchen, which he did for about forty years, he learned he could "talk to the God of pots and pans" all the time. Brother Lawrence's "method" entailed a "simple attentiveness, an habitual, loving turning of [his] eyes to God" at all times. The longer I have studied his conversations and letters, the more convinced I have become that his "secret" was simply to fall head over heels in love with God and let that transfuse and transform everything he was doing. In all he was doing, he says, he tried to maintain a "passionate regard" for God. "I turn my little omelette in the pan for love of God."[2]

You know what happens when you fall head over heels in love with someone. You can't get the beloved out of your mind. The beloved is present in every thought, shaping and directing every action.

The question is: How do we fall head over heels in love with God, the unseen-yet-everpresent One? Brother Lawrence reminds us that real love won't happen automatically. Infatuations may occur at first sight, but love that lasts will not. Lasting love requires attention to another. "We must know before we love, and to know God we must often think of him," says Brother Lawrence. "And when we love him we shall think of him all the more, for our heart is where our treasure is."[3]

What Is Contemplation?

Contemplation has to do with this loving attentiveness to God. It is based on the premise that God is immanent in the created order, particularly in the human order. Psalm 19 describes this:

The heavens are telling the glory of God;
    and the firmament proclaims his handiwork.
Day to day pours forth speech,
    and night to night declares knowledge.

Yet the psalmist recognized that it is not a matter of physical sound.

There is no speech, nor are there words;
    their voice is not heard;
yet their voice goes out through all the earth,
    and their words to the end of the world. (Ps 19:1-4 RSV)

Psalm 139 is a hymn about God's inescapable nearness. God knows us better than we know ourselves, the Psalmist exults in the first part (vv. 1-6). God is, and God will be wherever we are. There is nowhere God is not. Verse eight tells all:

If I ascend to heaven, thou art there!
    If I make my bed in Sheol, thou art there! (RSV)

We expect God to be in heaven, of course. What knocks us over is the discovery that God is in the depths, in hell, in Sheol, even if we *make* our bed there. The psalmist doesn't say, "If I trip and fall in"; he says, "If I *make* my bed there." And Sheol is by definition where God is not. There is nowhere we human beings go where the hound of heaven will not track us.

Is this not what the cross affirms? Our God has so fallen in love with us, he allows himself to be "edged out on a Cross" with us and for us. As Bonhoeffer phrased it, "God is beyond in the midst of our life." God shares our powerlessness and helplessness even to the point of dying our death.[4] The great fourteenth-century "social mystic" Catherine of Siena discovered that the "fiery abyss of charity" needed her as much as she needed him, for he acted as if he could not live without her, despite the fact that God is Life itself. The cross proves this. How else could one explain it? Only in this way—by recognizing that the Mad Lover has fallen in love with what he has made![5]

Catherine's comment calls to our attention the most basic premise underlying contemplation. What Rufus Jones has described as a "double search" goes on endlessly. Of necessity and by nature we seek the living God. "As the deer pants for streams of water, so my soul pants for you, O God. My soul thirsts for God, for the living God" (Ps 42:1-2). Is it not true, as Augustine prayed in his *Confessions,* "Thou hast made us for Thyself, to praise Thee, and our hearts are restless until they find rest in Thee"?[6] "The human heart is sensitive to God as the retina is to light waves," Rufus Jones wrote. "The soul possesses a native yearning for intercourse and companionship which takes it to God as naturally as the home instinct of the pigeon takes it to the place of its birth."[7]

At the same time God seeks us. Love never lets us go. It never gives up (see 1 Cor 13:8). The human will can shut the door and bar the windows and God will not knock the door down. God respects the freedom he has created us to enjoy. Nevertheless, he does not relent in his search. Is not the key point of our Lord's parable that the Father is watching? The Prodigal broke off all ties. He did not even dare, when he came to himself and decided to return home, to ask again to be received as a son. No, he would beg to be taken back as a hired hand. Yet, our Lord notes, "while he was still a long way off, his father saw him and was filled with compassion for him; he ran to his son, threw his arms around him and kissed him" (Lk 15:20). The father saw him from afar. He had never stopped watching. Day and night he had kept looking down the road, waiting, hoping, praying. So God does for all his errant ones.

Protestants have sometimes shunned the contemplative tradition as "works-righteousness." Contemplatives, they judge, try to "earn" salvation or make their own way to heaven. Nothing could be further from the truth. Over and over, the great spiritual guides will tirelessly remind you that contemplation depends on grace. We are respondents. We do not create the love or the grace by which we grow and develop. In the words of Jan Ruysbroeck, another of the brilliant fourteenth-century mystics, God's grace "pours into us in the unity of our higher powers and of our spirit" and, thus filled, "the higher powers flow out to become active in all virtues."[8] Our task is to open ourselves to God's gracious energies.

Contemplation may involve all of our faculties—seeing, hearing, tasting, touching, smelling, feeling, perceiving—but some images will appear more often than others. The seventeenth-century Anglican pastor and poet George Herbert prayed,

Teach me, my God and King,
In all things thee to see,
And what I do in anything,
To do it as for thee.

To this he added his own commentary on the contemplative mode.

A man that looks on glass,
On it may stay his eye;
Or if he pleaseth, through it pass,
And then the heav'n espy.[9]

Teilhard de Chardin, Jesuit philosopher and paleontologist whose efforts to reconcile faith and science have borne much fruit since his death in 1955, tried also to teach people to "see." Commenting on the phrase "In him we live and move and have our being" (Acts 17:28; a quotation from Epimenides), Teilhard argued that "by virtue of the Creation and, still more, of the incarnation, *nothing* here below is *profane* for those who know how to see."[10] The cosmic Christ constantly discloses himself in the universe so that "the great mystery of Christianity is not exactly the appearance, but the transparence, of God in the universe."[11]

Other contemplatives rely more on affective imagery and language. Bernard of Clairvaux, a towering political as well as religious figure in the twelfth century, spoke often of an experience of the "coming" of Christ. "I have *felt* that He was present; I remember later that He has been with me; I have sometimes even had a *presentiment* that He would come; but I have never *felt* His coming or His leaving" (emphasis mine).[12] Richard Rolle, a fourteenth-century English recluse and contemplative, described how, while sitting in chapel, he "suddenly *felt* within me an unwonted and pleasant fire" which became "ever more pleasing and full of heat" (emphasis mine).[13] John Wesley followed the same tradition when he articulated his experience in a Moravian meeting in Aldersgate. "About a quarter before nine, while [the Moravian preacher] was describing the change which God works in the heart through faith in Christ, I *felt* my heart strangely warmed. I *felt* I did trust in Christ, Christ alone for salvation; and an assurance was given me that he had taken away *my* sins, even *mine*, and saved *me* from the law of sin and death."[14]

The Eastern Christian contemplative tradition has resorted more to cognitive imagery and language, which have in turn expressed serious reservations about human ability to experience God or to describe such experience. The goal of Platonists was, of course, *gnōsis*—spiritual and not merely intellective knowledge. Both Christian and non-Christian Platonists coveted immediate, intuitive knowledge of the Divine. Christians, however, soon had reason to treat the claims of those calling themselves Gnostics with some suspicion. By the fourth century it had become common to look upon God in his essential reality as "beyond knowing." Gregory of Nyssa, using Moses' ascent of Mount Sinai as a paradigm, depicted the Christian journey toward perfection as a journey from darkness (of sin) to light (at baptism) through a cloud into utter darkness.[15] Human beings cannot look on God and live. Thus the highest experience results in unknowing rather than knowing. A Syrian Christian writing under the pseudonym of Dionysius, the Athenian who responded to Paul's preaching on Mars Hill, explained how Moses entered the divine dark to be united with God, who is "all-unknowable," by "the stilling of all knowing." So, too, do contemplatives desire "to come and, unseeing and unknowing, to see and to know Him that is beyond seeing and beyond knowing precisely by not seeing, by not knowing."[16]

The Contemplative Way

In the first few centuries, contemplatives developed a complete scheme concerning the path to perfection. The ultimate goal is usually expressed as union with God, but contemplatives may state the same hope and aspiration in a variety of ways. In an ultimate sense, of course, this hope lies beyond mortal existence. Contemplatives look toward life-beyond-life either in the sense of a future or of a transcendent state. Since God is life, whether we continue to *be* depends on participation in that life.

It is a fundamental conviction of contemplatives, however, that we may see God or be united with God, though fleetingly, while we are still living in this present state of existence. During the fourth century and after, hundreds flocked to the desert of Sinai to attain the vision of God Moses had on Mount Sinai. In his oft-sung hymn, "Jesus, the Very Thought of Thee," Bernard of Clairvaux articulated the heart's desire of generation after generation:

> Jesus, the very thought of Thee
>> With sweetness fills my breast;
> But sweeter far Thy face to see,
>> And in Thy presence rest.
> Jesus, our only joy be Thou,
>> As Thou our prize wilt be;
> Jesus, be Thou our glory now,
>> And through eternity.

Julian of Norwich, a remarkable fourteenth-century English saint and spiritual guide, explained that "the whole reason why we pray is to be united into the vision and contemplation of him to whom we pray, wonderfully rejoicing with reverent fear, and with so much sweetness and delight in him that we cannot pray at all except as he moves us at the time."[17] Numerous popular Protestant hymns express the same deep longing and reflect experiences remarkably like those of medieval contemplatives. Check Fanny Crosby's "I Am Thine, O Lord":

> I am Thine, O Lord, I have heard Thy voice,

And it told Thy love to me;
But I long to rise in the arms of faith,
And be closer drawn to Thee.[18]

How do we attain this goal? The desert Fathers observed early on that the key lies in *purity of heart*. Jesus said, "Blessed are the pure in heart, for they will see God" (Mt 5:8). What is purity of heart? Elsewhere in Matthew our Lord made it clear that he meant a character so transformed as to be downright good. Good trees bear good fruit (7:18). Not those who say, "Lord! Lord!" but those who do the will of the Father will enter the kingdom (7:21). The king will invite those who have fed the hungry, given drink to the thirsty, welcomed strangers, clothed the naked, visited the sick and imprisoned without even thinking they served Christ (25:31-40). As Søren Kierkegaard phrased it, "Purity of heart is to will one thing"—the good, what God wills.[19]

What can we do to attain purity of heart? The answer to this is: surrender, abandon ourselves, submit, yield, humble ourselves, give ourselves over to God. However apt we may be at education, self-understanding or formation, we cannot transform the impure into the pure, the sinful into the saintly, the unlovely into the lovely. God alone can do that. God's love alone can perform the miracle required. If we surrender, love will come in and cleanse and purify and transform.

Here is where our age and culture pose a problem for contemplatives. Our culture does not value and probably does not understand humility or meekness, which the contemplative tradition posits as the gateway to the spiritual road we must take if we would see God. In North America we laud aggressiveness, drive, *Looking Out for Number One* and *Winning through Intimidation* (the titles of Robert J. Ringer's best sellers). Persons who have experienced oppression—women and blacks or other minorities—have had enough of submission, yielding and meekness. They want empowerment rather than powerlessness.

Contemplatives, therefore, must be careful not to give the wrong impression in the call for surrender or submission. We do not abandon ourselves to injustice or oppression; in fact, not to human beings at all. Quite the contrary, we humble ourselves under the mighty hand of God, that in due time he may exalt us (1 Pet 5:6). We submit ourselves to God, trusting him to do with us far beyond our expectations. Humility or meekness, according to *The Cloud of Unknowing* (another outstanding fourteenth-century contemplative classic) "is nought else, but a true knowing and feeling of a [person's] self as one is." Two factors should evoke it: human frailty as a consequence of sin and "the over-abundant love and the worthiness of God in Himself; in beholding of which all nature quaketh, all clerks be fools, and all saints and angels be blind."[20]

The German and Dutch mystics understood this attitude in terms of Jesus' call to discipleship. "If anyone would come after me, let that person deny self and take up the cross and follow me" (Mk 8:34; my translation). Meister Eckhart spoke of "total self-detachment." He observed that the humble person has as much power over God as over self. "If this man were in hell, God would have to come down to him in hell," he added.[21] A "Friend of God," commenting on the beatitude "Blessed are the poor in spirit, for theirs is the kingdom of heaven" (Mt 5:3), spoke for the whole tradition in saying, "If [one] is really to attain to God, [one] must empty [oneself] of all self-action and permit God alone to act in [one]."[22] Evangelicals should not have difficulty with this kind of thinking. They too sing, "I surrender all. All to Jesus I surrender. All to him I freely give." The concept is one which came into this tradition by way of the Puritan search for genuine piety in the medieval contemplative tradition.[23]

"The Dark Night"

When we deny ourselves, we open ourselves to an invasion by the love of God that purifies and recreates us in the image of God. Although God's love is gentle, the process of purification and restoration will be painful, just as all growth is painful. The contemplatives speak of it as "the refiner's fire."

Americans, as is well known, do not like pain. We flee pain in every way possible. As Norman Cousins remarked in *Anatomy of an Illness*, "Americans are probably the most pain-conscious people on the face of the earth. For years we have had it drummed into us—in print, on radio, over television, in everyday conversation—that any hint of pain is to be banished as though it were the ultimate evil. As a result, we are becoming a nation of pillgrabbers and hypochondriacs, escalating the slightest ache into a searing ordeal."[24] There is, to be sure, avoidable pain, meaningless pain, senseless pain which we should try to escape. But there is also unavoidable pain and suffering which, if properly entered into, can help us grow in our relationship with God.

Many contemplatives have encouraged the use of what is called "compunction," a feeling of grief for sin or sorrow for the suffering of others, even the shedding of tears. They have meditated on the cross as a means of getting the heart in the right frame. The nameless "Friend of God" who composed *The Book of the Poor in Spirit* spoke for many contemplatives when he said that "Nothing brings [human beings] closer to God than acceptance of suffering" because it uproots ingratitude and opens us to God, who is present to us above all in suffering. As God comes, he delivers us "from all that is not God."[25] Thomas Kelly, who had reason to know the meaning of his words, said, "The heart is stretched through suffering, and enlarged." The cross is painful. "Yet God, out of the pattern of His own heart, has planted the Cross along the road to holy obedience."[26]

Contemplatives do not have to seek suffering. If we are alive, it will find us. And the more love sandpapers our hearts, the more it quickens us to suffering. Was it not this which lured Francis of Assisi into a love affair with "Lady Poverty," or commanded Catherine of Genoa to tend to the "poorest of the poor" in the Pammatone hospital? Mother Teresa, one of the modern imitators of Francis, has said, "One cannot expect to become a saint without paying the price, and the price is much renunciation, much temptation, much struggle and persecution, and all sorts of sacrifices."[27]

Human beings experience pain in a variety of ways and from different sources. The deepest pain is the pain of intimacy with another person. The deeper the bond between persons, the greater the pain of separation. Those who have suffered broken friendships or divorce or death will know what I mean. Many persons never develop intimate relationships with others precisely because it is too painful; they cannot or will not take the risk. Is this not what also holds many in check in their development of intimacy with God? Their pain threshold is too low to undertake a journey into "the dark night of the soul."

The classic by that title (by John of the Cross) may appear too severe and stereotyped to guide many toward contemplation today. I wonder, however, whether his ardent desire for purity of heart can be dismissed. John envisioned two nights actually. One is "the night of the senses" and the other "the night of the spirit." To attain transparency of character we must pass through both. In the first, we may play a part in the purification of the senses; but in the second, love must take control, wiping out the last vestiges of the self-centeredness which prevents us from becoming one with God. As fire consumes a log and turns it into itself, so God's love ignites the human soul and transforms it into love itself.[28]

Climbing the Ladder of Love

More must be said about love as the means by which God accomplishes his purposes. Jesus himself summed up all the commandments in two: "Love the Lord your God with all your heart and with all your soul and with all your mind and with all your strength" and "Love your neighbor as yourself" (Mk 12:29-31). The apostle Paul reduced it to the second (Rom 13:9), presumably because neighbor-love demonstrates love of God in deed rather than in word only. The contemplative perspective revolves around this very thing. "The message of hope the contemplative offers you," wrote Thomas Merton to another Cistercian, "is not that you need to find your way through the jungle of language and problems that today surround God: but that whether you understand or not, God loves you, is present in you, lives in you, dwells in you, calls you, saves you, and offers you an understanding and light which are like nothing you ever found in books or heard in sermons."[29] Contemplatives can speak in abstruse and unintelligible imagery and language, but most of them have reduced the whole to this profoundly simple word: "God loves you. Love God back."

Bernard of Clairvaux has marked out four stages in the love of God. The first is *love of self for self's sake.* Bernard wisely observed that we cannot love others unless we first love ourselves. Unless we love our neighbors, moreover, we cannot love God. Yet not even love of self is possible without the prior love of God. Love is a natural affection which God has poured into us. As John says, "We love because he first loved us" (1 Jn 4:19). The second is *love of God for self's sake.* Here we do not rise far above the first level, for we still love for selfish reasons. In time of trouble God comes to our side and thus "melts us down" in gratitude. If we experience God's love and mercy in recurrent troubles, Bernard continues, we may begin to move to the third state—*love of God for God's sake.* We love God not because of what God does for us but "because we have tasted ourselves and know how gracious the Lord is." At this level we love purely and without self-interest. Many other contemplatives viewed this as the highest love human beings could attain to, but Bernard added one more stage—*love of self for God's sake.* To love self in this way means to put oneself completely at God's disposal, to merge one's will into God's, to surrender completely. Bernard doubted whether even martyrs attained love of this degree. It happens only to souls "loosed from their bodies" and "immersed completely in that sea of endless light and bright eternity."[30]

How do we grow in love? Contemplatives would say, virtually in unison, *by means of God's love.* God, Bernard wrote, "is both prime mover of our love and final end. He is himself our human love's occasion; He also gives the power to love, and brings desire to consummation. He is himself the Lovable in his essential being, and gives himself to be the object of our love. He wills our love for him to issue in our bliss, not to be void and vain. His love both opens up the way for ours and is our love's reward."[31] From the time of Origen (185-254) contemplatives have borrowed the imagery of the Song of Songs to explain the love affair with which God engages the human soul. A thirteenth-century Flemish Beguine named Hadewijch composed a complete set of poems in stanzas depicting her painful experience in the love of God. Threatened by the Inquisition, she felt forsaken at times by Love, whom she regularly addresses as *she.* At a particularly vulnerable moment Hadewijch asked,

Whereabouts is Love? I find her nowhere.
Love has denied me all love.
Had it ever happened to me by Love
That I lived for a moment
In her affection, supposing I did,
I would have sought amnesty in her fidelity.
Now I must keep silence, suffer, and face
Sharp judgments ever anew.[32]

Still she maintained a dogged trust in Love. "In serving Love one cannot lose,/ Although it is true that she brings help late."[23] Her advice to those plagued by doubt and fear as she was, therefore, was to:

Fix all your thought

On the Love of God who created you.
Commend all your being to Love;
So shall you heal all torments
And pains, and you shall fear nothing,
And shall not flee from adversity in anything[34]

The intimacy and intensity of the prayers of medieval contemplatives may shock moderners, accustomed to associating such talk with Gothic romances and soap operas. Exulted Richard Rolle:

O my love! O my Honey! O my Harp! O my psalter and canticle all the day! When will you heal my grief? O root of my heart, when will You come to me so that You may raise up with You my spirit, looking upward for You? For You see that I am wounded vitally by Your super-brilliant beauty, and my lassitude does not release me. On the contrary, it rises greater and greater in its growth and present penalties press me and fight me, so that I hasten to You from Whom alone I hope for my comfort and the remedy about to be seen.[35]

Although secular taste has made contemplatives in later times more discreet about language, the intimacy revealed here has not and cannot disappear, because it is crucial for growth in love. Transparency is essential for the cultivation of an intimate personal relationship with another. Responses which are natural for love must create the bond which unites heart to heart. Even in Protestantism, therefore, we will meet with similar expressions of longing and desire. "Jesus, Lover of my soul," pleaded Charles Wesley, "Let me to thy bosom fly, . . . Thou, O Christ, art all I want; More than all in Thee I find: . . . Thou of life the fountain art, Freely let me take of Thee; Spring Thou up within my heart, Rise to all eternity." Another hymnist professes,

My Jesus, I love Thee, I know Thou art mine,
For Thee all the follies of sin I resign;
My gracious Redeemer, my Saviour art Thou;
If ever I loved Thee, my Jesus, 'tis now.[37]

Thomas Merton's writings often echo the lyrics of love. In his journal on September 26, 1948, he tells how "the bridegroom of Lady Compassion" overflowed with love.

Love sails me around the house. I walk two steps on the ground and four steps in the air. It is love. It is consolation. I love God. Love carries me all around. I don't want to do anything but love. And when the bell rings it is like pulling teeth to make myself shift because of that love, secret love, hidden love, obscure love, down inside me and outside me where I don't care to talk about it. Anyway I don't have the time or the energy to discuss such matters. I have only time for eternity, which is to say for love, love, love. Maybe Saint Teresa would like to have me snap out of it but it is pure, I tell you; I am not attached to it (I hope) and it is love and it gives me soft punches all the time in the center of my heart. Love is pushing me around the monastery, love is kicking me all around like a gong. I tell you, love is the only thing that makes it possible for me to continue to tick.[38]

Communion with God

At the heart of the contemplative approach is communion, communication or conversation with God—prayer. Prayer may take a variety of forms, beginning with vocal expression and extending all the way to the ecstasy of union with God. The medieval contemplatives envisioned three stages. Teresa of Avila, the sixteenth-century Carmelite whom Pope Paul VI honored for her instruction in prayer as the first woman "Doctor of the Church," added a fourth.

The first stage consists of a mental exercise wherein persons seek to know God cognitively through reason, human learning and study of the Scriptures. According to Teresa, prayer at this level is like hauling water out of a cistern with a bucket; it requires discipline and determination on our part. Teresa herself spent twenty years learning how to pray, and so we should not be discouraged if we find it laborious and seem to make no progress.

The second stage uses the heart more than the head. Here persons of limited learning may surpass scholars, for grace begins to lend greater assistance. Teresa described this "prayer of quiet" as water being drawn up by a water wheel; we make some effort, but much less than in mental prayer. Walter Hilton called it "love on fire with devotion."[39] Affect plays a prominent role in this kind of prayer. Medieval monks developed a method of "reading" or meditating on Scriptures, on which Christian meditation has always turned. Reading a passage of Scripture, they would pause at length to reflect on its word for them, and enter the text, as it were, through imagination.

In the sixteenth century Ignatius Loyola perfected this approach in his *Spiritual Exercises*. He set forth a plan for a four-week retreat entailing meditation on human sin and need, the life of Christ, Christ's death and the resurrection, and the kingdom of Christ. The object is, through the use of the imagination, to have the mind of Christ (Phil 2:5) formed in you. Many of our grandmothers, without knowing they were contemplatives, prayed in their rocking chairs in much the same way. Rocking back and forth with their Bibles open on their laps, they asked the Word to speak to them and their concerns for their families or friends. In the fast-paced day in which we live, unfortunately, most persons have given up rocking-chair prayer.

Although earlier contemplatives envisioned the next level as the last, Teresa interjected what she described as a "sleep of the faculties" before the final stage. Here God's grace pours into us like water from a river or spring and we experience "incomparably greater" pleasure, sweetness and delight as "the water of grace rises to the very neck of the soul."[40] One already experiences union with God, but still retains enough awareness of self to know what is happening.

The final stage of prayer is what Hugo of St. Victor labeled "contemplation" and Walter Hilton described as "love on fire with contemplation." This level involves both cognition and affection, according to Hilton, but now the contemplative knows and loves God perfectly, with pure mind and heart. The experience depends entirely on grace. The Holy Spirit enters with "a soft, sweet burning love" and unites one with God.[41] Contemplatives would normally speak about mystical union as a momentary experience, but there is a remarkable exception in Blaise Pascal's *Memorial*. Using the single word *fire*, Pascal described an experience which lasted about two hours!

> God of Abraham, God of Isaac, God of Jacob,
>   not of the philosophers and the learned.
> Certitude, certitude; feeling, joy, peace.
>   God of Jesus Christ
>   "My God and Thy God"
>   Thy God shall be my God.
>   The world forgot and all save God.
> We lay hold of Him only through the teaching of the Gospel.[42]

Teresa of Avila distinguished rapture from union in this degree of prayer. Rapture, she concluded, "is much more beneficial than union" in its effects, for the soul is seized up to heaven, where the Lord reveals to it the secrets of the kingdom.[43] Others, beginning with the apostle Paul (2 Cor 12:1-10), have spoken of rapture also without distinguishing so precisely. Bernard of Clairvaux, the premier guide of the contemplative tradition, confessed he had had the experience which he could not truly describe. "The mind is drawn along by the ineffable sweetness of the word and, as it were, it is stolen from itself or, better, it is rapt and remains out of itself there to enjoy the Word." The meaning of such an experience can only be taught by grace.[44]

Contemplation in a World of Action

Before concluding this discussion, I must speak to the doubts many persons have about the relevance of contemplation in a world of action. Since the reformers closed the monasteries in the sixteenth century, Protestants have regularly criticized contemplatives for abandonment of society and charged them with failing to exercise proper responsibility. Indeed, until recent years, they have disputed vigorously the validity of the contemplative vocation. Contemplatives spend too much time "saving their own souls," too little time serving humankind.

In the past few decades contemplatives too have gone through some soul-searching about their vocations. More than any other person, Thomas Merton, a Trappist monk of the Abbey of Gethsemani in Kentucky, has wrestled agonizingly with the question of a contemplative vocation and proven that it not only has retained its relevance but that its significance has increased. At the center of the malaise of Western society, he concluded, is the fact that moderners leave no place "for wisdom that seeks truth for its own sake, that seeks the fullness of being, that seeks to rest in an intuition of the very ground of all being." In a world such as this contemplatives have a mission. "The mission of the contemplative in this world of massive conflict and collective unreason is to seek the true way of unity and peace, without succumbing to the illusion of withdrawal into a realm of abstraction from which unpleasant realities are simply excluded by the force of will." Very often "the ordinary active and ethical preoccupations of Christians make them forget this deeper and more contemplative dimension of the

Christian way."[45] Pursuit of this vocation turned Merton's eyes East ward to study oriental wisdom. Those who know the sixties will remember Merton as one of America's most perceptive social prophets.

One of Merton's special contributions was to show that contemplation does not necessitate a cloistered life. What it involves, rather, is "a special dimension of inner discipline and experience, a certain integrity and fullness of personal development, which are not compatible with a purely external, alienated, busy-busy existence."[46] Persons engaged in all kinds of occupations may be contemplatives. Dag Hammarskjöld, secretary general of the United Nations, surprised many when he left behind deeply interiorized reflections on his own demanding public life. "The longest journey," be wrote, "is the journey inwards."[47] Yet he could speak about the immense reward from it.

Calm is the soul that is emptied of all self,
In a restful harmony—
This happiness is here and now,
In the eternal moment of co-inherence.
A happiness within you—but not yours.[48]

Contemplation tempered and tendered him personally. "Do you really have 'feelings' any longer for anybody or anything except yourself—or even that?" he asked. Then he answered, "Without the strength of a personal commitment, your experience of others is at most aesthetic." But he had to confess, "Yet, to-day, even such a maimed experience brought you into touch with a portion of spiritual reality which revealed your utter poverty."[49]

One doesn't have to search long to find contemplatives who have made a profound impact on their society and age. For the eighteenth century, John Woolman stands out. Reared in a devout Quaker home, he became sensitized early on to all human and animal life. Writing a bill of sale for a black female slave further quickened his conscience. When he began traveling around the American colonies as a minister in 1746, he could not help but notice the plight of slaves.

For the remainder of his life (he died in 1772) he spent about one month out of every year entreating his fellow makers to free their slaves. He was what I would call a quiet revolutionary. When he attended Quaker meetings, he quietly laid upon them the burden of his heart. If he stayed in a home where there were slaves, in the morning he would press some money in the hands of his host to give to a trusted slave with a view to purchasing freedom. He stopped wearing dyed suits because the dye for making men's suits was produced by slave labor. He refused to eat sugar, rum and molasses manufactured in the West Indies because they involved slave labor. Sensitive person that he was, however, he worried lest too many persons follow his example and thus inflict greater hurt on those he wanted to help. After 1763 he refused to ride on horseback or in conveyances because slaves could not do so. In the matter of slavery and in other areas John Woolman began to see that injustice comes about less from deliberate and planned effort than it does from unthinking and a lack of sensitivity. If we knew the love of God in a genuine sense, we would not desire comforts and conveniences, what he called "superfluities," without being aware of how our desire might cause injury to another.

There is a reciprocal relationship between contemplation and action. Contemplatives who enter into the world in its press and struggle may find their spirituality deepening and their personal perceptions maturing. When Evelyn Underhill, a noted student of the mystics, asked Baron Friedrich von Hugel to serve as her spiritual guide, he directed her first to spend two afternoons a week visiting the poor. "If properly entered into and persevered with," he explained, it "will discipline, mortify, deepen, and quiet you" and "as it were, distribute your blood—some of your blood—away from your brain, where too much is lodged at present."[50] Rufus Jones warned that "to withdraw from the human press and struggle and seek only the selfish thrill of individual salvation is the way of spiritual danger."[51]

At the same time contemplation must inform social service and action if they are to have depth and meaning. "When action and contemplation dwell together, filling our whole life because we are moved in all things by the Spirit of God," Merton has remarked, "then we are spiritually mature."[52] Contemplation purifies our intention. It gathers up inner resources which can enable us to face the difficult tasks. It transforms our vision of the world. It orders our priorities.

Notes

[1]Thomas R. Kelly, *A Testament of Devotion* (New York: Harper & Row, 1941), pp. 38-43.

[2]Brother Lawrence, *The Practice of the Presence of God*, trans. E. M. Blaiklock (Nashville:

Thomas Nelson, 1981), pp. 45, 85.

[3]Ibid., p. 52.

[4]Dietrich Bonhoeffer, *Letters and Papers from Prison,* enlarged ed., ed. Eberhard Bethge (New York: Macmillan, 1953), p. 282.

[5]Catherine of Siena, *The Dialogue,* trans. Suzanne Noffke, Classics of Western Spirituality (New York: Paulist Press, 1980), p. 325.

[6]Augustine *Confessions* 1.1.1.

[7]Rufus Jones, *The Double Search* (London: Headley Brothers, 1906), pp. 86-87.

[8]Jan Ruysbroeck, *Adornment of the Spiritual Marriage,* trans. C. A. Wynschenck Dom (London: J. M. Dent & Sons, 1916), p. 55.

[9]George Herbert, *The Country Parson and the Temple,* Classics of Western Spirituality (New York: Paulist Press, 1981), p. 311.

[10]Teilhard de Chardin, *Le Milieu Divin* (London: Collins, 1957), p. 66.

[11]Ibid., p. 131.

[12]Bernard, "Sermon LXXXIII on the Song of Songs," in *Varieties of Mystic Experience,* ed. Elmer O'Brien (New York: Mentor-Omega, 1964), p. 105.

[13]Richard Rolle, "The Fire of Love," in O'Brien, *Varieties,* p. 133.

[14]John Wesley, *Journal,* in *John Wesley,* ed. Albert C Outler, A Library of Protestant Thought (New York: Oxford University Press, 1964), p. 66.

[15]Gregory of Nyssa *Life of Moses* 163.

[16]Pseudo-Dionysius, *The Mystical Theology,* in O'Brien, *Varieties,* pp. 72-73.

[17]Julian of Norwich, *Showings,* trans. Edmund Colledge and James Walsh, Classics of Western Spirituality (New York: Paulist Press, 1978), p. 254.

[18]Compare to E. Glenn Hinson, "Southern Baptist and Medieval Spirituality: Surprising Similarities," *Cistercian Studies* 20 (1985), pp 224-36.

[19]Søren Kierkegaard, *Purity of Heart,* trans. Douglas V. Steere (New York: Harper & Row, 1956).

[20]Evelyn Underhill, ed., *The Cloud of Unknowing,* 6th ed. (London: John M. Watkins, 1956), pp. 100-101.

[21]Meister Eckhart, *The Essential Sermons, Commentaries, Treatises and Defense,* trans. Edmund Colledge and Bernard McGinn, Classics of Western Spirituality (New York: Paulist Press, 1981), p. 190.

[22]C. F. Kelley, ed. and trans., *The Book of the Poor in Spirit* (New York: Harper & Bros., n.d.), p. 168.

[23]See E. Glenn Hinson, "Reassessing the Puritan Heritage in Worship/Spirituality: A Search for a Method," *Worship* 53 (July 1979), pp. 318-26; "Puritan Spirituality," in *Protestant Spiritual Traditions,* ed. Frank C. Senn (New York: Paulist Press, 1986), pp. 165-82.

[24]Norman Cousins, *Anatomy of an Illness as Perceived by the Patient* (New York & London: W. W. Norton, 1979), p. 89.

[25]Kelley, *Book of the Poor in Spirit,* p. 225.

[26]Kelly, *Testament of Devotion,* p. 71.

[27]Mother Teresa, *The Love of Christ: Spiritual Counsels* (San Francisco: Harper & Row, 1982), p. 21.

[28]John of the Cross, *The Dark Night of the Soul,* trans. E. Allison Peers (Garden City, N.Y.: Doubleday, 1959), p. 127.

[29]Thomas Merton, *The Hidden Ground of Love,* ed. William Shannon (New York: Farrar, Straus and Giroux, 1985), p. 156.

[30]Bernard of Clairvaux *On the Love of God* 8-10.

[31]Bernard of Clairvaux *On the Love of God* 7.

[32]Hadewijch, *The Complete Works,* trans. Mother Columba Hart, Classics of Western Spirituality (New York: Paulist Press, 1980), p. 228.

[33]Ibid., p. 255.

[34]Ibid., p. 330.

[35]Richard Rolle, *The Fire of Love,* trans. M. L. Del Mastro (Garden City, N.Y.: Doubleday Image Books, 1981), p. 111.

[36]Charles Wesley, "Jesus, Lover of My Soul," *Baptist Hymnal,* ed. Walter Hines Sims (Nashville: Convention Press, 1956), pp. 156-58.

[37]William R. Featherstone, "My Jesus, I Love Thee," Sims, *Hymnal,* p. 289.

[38]Thomas Merton, *The Sign of Jonas* (London: Burns & Oates, 1953), p. 116.

[39]Walter Hilton, *The Stairway of Perfection,* trans. M. L. Del Mastro (Garden City, N.Y.: Doubleday Image Books, 1979), p. 71.

[40]Teresa of Avila, *Autobiography,* trans. & ed. E. Allison Peers (Garden City, N.Y.: Doubleday Image Books, 1960), p. 163.

[41]Hilton, *Stairway,* p. 71.

[42]Blaise Pascal, *Pensées,* trans. H. F. Stewart (New York: Random House/Modern Library, 1941), p. 363.

[43]Teresa, *Autobiography,* p. 189.

[44]Bernard of Clairvaux, "Sermon 85 on the Song of Songs," in O'Brien, *Varieties,* p. 106.

[45]Thomas Merton, *Faith and Violence* (Notre Dame, Ind.: University of Notre Dame Press, 1968), pp. 216-17, 221, 223.

[46]Thomas Merton, *Contemplation in a World of Action* (Garden City, N.Y.: Doubleday, 1971), p. 157.

[47]Dag Hammarskjöld, *Markings,* trans. W. H. Auden & Leif Sjöberg (London: Faber & Faber, 1964), p. 65.

[48]Ibid., p. 51.

[49]Ibid., p. 58.

[50]Cited by Douglas V. Steere, *Together in Solitude* (New York: Crossroad, 1982), p. 57.

[51]Rufus Jones, "Our Social Task and What It Demands" (pamphlet).

[52]Thomas Merton, *No Man Is an Island* (Garden City, N.Y.: Doubleday Image Books, 1967), p. 65.

A Lutheran Response
Gerhard O. Forde

T HE CONTEMPLATIVE VIEW GIVES US ANOTHER INTERESTING IN-
sight into the promises and perils of our speaking about sanctification. Generally speaking, the history of the church shows
that mystical and contemplative views tend to become prominent at
certain characteristic times. When the "old gods" become oppressive,
when theology becomes bogged down in abstract objectivist descriptions and hair-splitting scholastic definitions, or when its ethics become too legalistic and heteronomous, or perhaps when the gods are
eclipsed by an arid scientific and technological society, there is a tendency to take refuge in "the inner life" where we are supposed to be
able to commune more immediately with God. The contemplative
knows at least one thing that is often overlooked by more objectivist
or law-oriented talk about sanctification. The contemplative knows that
the affective dimension holds the key to our real growth. Love is the
ultimate motor and goal of sanctification.

Once having said that, however, the trouble starts again and perhaps
even to a more intense degree. The trouble is that the talk about sanctification gets even more highly inflated because the ante gets raised,
so to speak. Rather than a more or less modest goal of good works,
there is once again a good deal of talk about "a path to perfection,"

"the ascent of the mountain" (Sinai, Carmel or Zion), toward the ultimate goal of "union with God" and such matters. Now supposedly it is less onerous because it is supposed to be more *inner* than outer, more a matter of *contemplation* than action.

But the difficulty is that one sets up pretty much the same sort of scheme as what had come to plague the *outer* life. In the very act of *describing* the contemplative life one does pretty much the same sort of thing one does in trying to describe the active life. The goal, Hinson says, is union with God, though contemplatives can describe it in a variety of ways. But then comes the question: How do we attain this goal? Answer: "The key lies in purity of heart"; "those who have fed the hungry, given drink to the thirsty, welcomed strangers and clothed the naked." What can we do to get purity of heart? "Surrender, abandon ourselves, submit, yield, humble yourself, give ourselves over to God." "If we surrender, love will come in and cleanse and purify and transform," and so on.

Now there are at least two problems with this conception of the matter. The first problem is the same old one we have noted in the other views. One can hardly escape the clutches of practical Pelagianism once again. The test case always comes when someone raises the nasty question, what if it doesn't work? What if love doesn't seem to "come in and cleanse and purify and transform?" What if I just seem to remain the same old impure-hearted person no matter how much I try? Then it can only be, I suppose, that I have not "surrendered" or "abandoned myself" or whatever it is that I am supposed to do. Once again, it does not really make much difference that contemplatives all say this occurs by the absolutely free motion of divine grace. The language all indicates that if it doesn't work, it's my fault. The more it is insisted that grace is absolutely free against the background of such language, the more everything will depend on *my* action. Since I can't blame grace, I can only blame myself. Contemplatives who keep protesting that the way they propose is not practical Pelagianism but granted only by grace never seem to understand that it is the very use of the language itself that is betraying the game. When you come back from the mountain and tell your admirers that the trip was totally by grace, but then answer questions on how to make the trip by talking about surrender, humility, self-abandonment and all sorts of spiritual exercises, the emphasis has slipped from grace to human effort. The protestations about grace appear simply an anti-Pelagian codicil, a mostly verbal protest whose substance is not apparent.

The second though related problem, more peculiar to the contemplative way, is the turn to the inner life itself. Martin Luther thought that the turn to the inner life (enthusiasm or "God-within-ism") was the essence of the Fall. It is the devil who wants always to cast us back on our own resources, tearing us away from the *external* Word and sacrament. To be sure, the external must be internally appropriated, but salvation comes *from without*, calls us out of our own internality and will impress itself upon our inner lives only to the degree that it comes absolutely and totally from without. We seem to have a desperately difficult time believing this. We are always collapsing inward upon ourselves. We are always turned inward *(curvatus in se)*. The self is a black hole endlessly sucking everything into itself and contemplating its own case. That is why the use of language in the contemplative way, no matter how much it wants to insist on grace, always turns to its opposite. The self is simply cast back upon itself and never gets out.

So it is that the language of grace must be a language that comes totally from without. It does not call on the old self, not even the inner life of the old self, to somehow traverse a new way. It announces him who is the Way. It is thus a use of language which does not call on the old self to "surrender"; rather it is a use of language which through its very givenness *slays* the old by the absolute unconditionality of the gift itself. As we saw in Ferguson's essay, the Word does not call on our old beings to die. It simply announces that we *have* died, and sanctification occurs to the degree that we get used to that fact.

Once again the talk about sanctification is long on description and faulty in execution. The contemplative is right in putting so much weight on the affective side of the matter. Love is the source and goal of sanctification, but the only way to bring that about is to simply announce, "I love you." The word of grace must bring the old unlovely and unloving existence to an end by the sheer strength of the promise, the gift, which breaks into our dreary lives and just announces flat-out that the old has passed away and the new is here. There will simply be no true sanctification unless that is done. And what sanctification there is will be our getting used to the shock of such grace.

A Reformed Response
Sinclair B. Ferguson

UNLIKE THE OTHER ESSAYS IN THIS SYMPOSIUM, DR. HINson's impressive study inevitably spans all the Christian centuries. The contemplative view of holiness seems to transcend denominational (Lutheran, Wesleyan) or theological (Pentecostal, Reformed) boundaries.

Dr. Hinson mentions some of the best-known exponents of the contemplative life, noting that it need not be antithetical to the life of action. For this reason one also discovers something akin to the contemplative spirit in the Reformed tradition, for example, in many of the Puritans and their followers. This illustrates the important point that the contemplative tradition is not theologically monolithic. Consequently any discussion of it (as perhaps of any of the traditions represented in this symposium!) must carry a theological health warning: "These comments do not apply to all members of this tradition!" My aim in responding to Dr. Hinson's exposition is to indicate some of the distinctives in the emphases of Reformed Christians who might from a certain perspective be described as contemplatives themselves.

Reformed spirituality differs from one strand of the contemplative tradition in its epistemology. It recognizes the biblical doctrine of the incomprehensibility of God (he cannot be known exhaustively, as he knows himself); but it stresses that true knowledge of God is ours through revelation. The central strand of Reformed thought, therefore, does not employ the quasi-mystical language of "unknowing" which (especially from Pseudo-Dionysius) appears in the contemplative tradition's search for knowledge of God's essence. Rather, it stresses that God has come near and accommodated himself to us in Christ and through Scripture. We come to know him, not by rising above rational thought, but by submitting our understanding and life to his self-revelation. "The word is near you; it is in your mouth and in your heart" (Rom 10:8) is the starting place for Reformed contemplation of God. We neither ascend into heaven or descend into the deep in order to know God (Rom 10:6-7). We meet God in the words of Scripture. In Scripture (not beyond it), says Hebrews 12:5, God speaks (present tense) as a Father to his children (gracious relationship).

In this context one may notice a feature of the language of, for example, the seventeenth-century Scottish pastor-theologian-correspondent Samuel Rutherford, who from one point of view might easily be claimed for the contemplative tradition. He approaches God through the historical Christ, scripturally understood as once crucified, now exalted. By contrast the contemplative tradition often seems to Reformed Christians to bypass the central apostolic categories through which the significance of his historically conditioned redemptive work is to be understood. To the Reformed observer of the full-blown contemplative tradition, it often seems that Christ's ministry serves as a mirror for contemplation in order to lead to God. But it is insufficiently stressed that what he has done actually gives us access to God (Eph 2:18).

In Reformed theology and its view of Scripture, the gospel is not: "God loves you. Love God back," as Dr. Hinson suggests of the contemplative tradition. Rather it is: "God was reconciling the world to himself in Christ, not counting men's sins against them. . . . God made him who had no sin to be sin for us . . . that in him we might become the righteousness of God" (2 Cor 5:18, 21). The appropriate response is not primarily "Love God back," but "Be reconciled to God" and "Believe in the Lord Jesus" (2 Cor 5:20; Acts 16:31).

It is because of what we believe about Christ—that the cross is to be interpreted as atonement, propitiation, ransom and reconciliation—

that we are constrained by Christ's love. Here no biblical statement is more vital than Paul's words in 2 Corinthians 5:14, "because we are convinced that one died for all" (that is, because we believe this to be the interpretation of Christ's death). The response to which we are summoned cannot adequately be described as *contemplating*. It needs to be *believing*.

While the contemplative tradition places much emphasis on Christ's humanity and passion as such, Reformed Christianity places central emphasis on the transaction which took place in the incarnate Son of God bearing the judgment of his Holy Father against man's sin (Rom 8:32; Gal 3:13). Bypass this, it insists, and there is no access to, and therefore no real knowledge of, God.

I remember being taken as a child to see Salvador Dali's famous painting "Christ of St. John of the Cross," displayed, as now, in the Art Gallery of my native city of Glasgow, Scotland. Dali portrayed Christ on the cross from the vantage point of above and slightly to the rear. Beneath is the Sea of Galilee and the disciples with their boats. The single most striking feature of the painting is this: the cross is *floating between heaven and earth, but it is not planted on the earth.* Of course, Dali ought not to be taken as the most reliable commentator on the theology of such a monumental figure as John of the Cross. But his painting indicates precisely why Reformed theology has sometimes felt uneasy about the contemplative tradition's tendency to interpret Christ mystically rather than historically, and in ideal rather than in biblical-theological categories.

Dr. Hinson suggests that Protestants have sometimes (often?) misunderstood the contemplative tradition to be a form of salvation by works, with no place given to grace. It is true that often the Protestant tradition understands only its own language. But there is a reason for such a response: in Scripture, the grace of God is manifested *in Christ's work*—specifically interpreted as propitiation, reconciliation, redemption—wrought in order to be received by faith. Contemplation is not the way of salvation; atonement is.

Direct knowledge of God's essence is sought only by fools, Calvin wrote boldly. What did he mean by such apparently audacious words? He was dominated, here as elsewhere, by his concern to safeguard the atoning work of Christ. However much he might admire the sometimes awe-inspiring devotion of the mystical path, he saw that whenever it transforms the biblical emphasis on propitiation to be received by faith into contemplation expressed in love, it bypasses what is central to biblical revelation. Of course—and this must be heavily underscored—these are not necessarily antithetical; they may (and should) exist together. And certainly in some exponents of the contemplative tradition, as well as in the Reformed tradition, they do. Where emphasis on atonement as the means to the knowledge of God is lacking, mystical contemplation alone is a less than biblical pursuit of the knowledge of God. It is this balance that Reformed Christians look for in the contemplative tradition, but do not always think they hear with sufficient clarity.

A Wesleyan Response
Laurence W. Wood

[handwritten note: There is a lack of discussion on how we fit into this chapter of history the church]

AWESLEYAN BELIEVER WILL FIND LITTLE TO DISAGREE WITH IN Hinson's contemplative view of spirituality. It is well known that John Wesley was highly influenced by the mystic tradition, even though the extent of that influence is debatable.

Wesley, however, disavowed ever embracing mystical theology except that he agreed with its emphasis on the inwardness of faith and a devotional relationship to Christ *(Works,* 10:391). His rejection of mystical theology centered around several points.

To begin with, he believed the mystics bypassed the proper means of grace because of their minimizing of the importance of holy communion, church attendance and service to others.

Second, their concept of grace was allegedly too subjective. Wesley believed this interpretation of salvation might distort the faith into an enclave of religious individuals isolated from the world. The result would be a loss of the meaning of the church as a community of believers.

Third, Wesley specifically rejected what he believed was a setting aside of the priority of Scripture. Because of the heavy emphasis on a direct and unmediated individualistic relationship to God, Wesley believed mystical theology carried with it the implication that the church has as many Bibles as mystics. It is in this context of rejecting a privatized and individualistic brand of Christianity that Wesley says there is "no holiness but social holiness" (*Works*, 14:321).

In a letter to his brother on November 23, 1736, Wesley says that the writings of the mystics had almost at one point in his life caused him to make a "shipwreck of the faith." Wesley thus resisted this subjectivistic tendency, though he was nonetheless influenced by it. In fact, Wesley's view of sanctification was so obviously mystical in many respects that frequently he was labeled a papist. He was also called a papist because union with Christ means that one's salvation inherently is distinguished by the outward sign of good works. This dual emphasis is the Anglo-Catholic background to Wesley's theology. Wesley had tried both the way of the mystic and the way of good works. The ideal of a holy life Wesley had learned largely from the mystic tradition. Wesley had assumed this holiness could be achieved by good works. Hence in 1729 John and Charles Wesley, along with about twenty-five others, formed the Oxford Club. Their intent in some measure was to earn salvation through their good deeds, as helping the poor and sick and visiting prisoners. Wesley denied himself during this period of time some of the basic necessities of life in an ascetic-like manner.

In 1735, Wesley sailed to Georgia with General Oglethorpe to be a missionary to the Native Americans, but he discovered that he did not himself have the assurance of salvation. Neither mysticism nor good deeds had saved him. On May 24, 1738, Wesley happened into a home where some believers had gathered together for worship. While he was sitting in that small group, Wesley felt his "heart strangely warmed" as someone was reading from Martin Luther's preface to the Book of Romans. From this point on Wesley affirmed the Reformation doctrine of justification by faith through grace alone. Wesley's high-church theology (which was Anglo-Catholic and Arminian) was forever linked to the Reformation theology of grace.

The uniqueness of Wesley's contribution to the Christian tradition lies in his synthesis of the mystical ideal of holiness (loving God with all the heart) with the Reformation doctrine of evangelical grace. One is justified by faith as the Reformers preached, but one can also experience mystical union with God through the means of grace by faith alone. This emphasis on the means of grace (especially the Scriptures) protects faith from a pantheistic subjectivism in which union with God happens in a direct and unmediated manner that fails to preserve the distinction between God and his creation.

Hinson does not address all these possible implications of mystical theology, and I am sure that he would find some of Wesley's remarks overstated. However, it should be kept in mind that Wesley did have to address some problems created by the spiritual and mystical enthusiasts of his day. More relevant to the present discussion is, what role does the means of grace play for Hinson and his understanding of mystical theology? It would have been helpful if Hinson had addressed this issue more directly.

Finally, I would like to commend Hinson for his mystical writing style that in itself captures the warm, personal and affective style of the mystics with their intense subjective feelings of God's presence in their lives. Some may find the subjectivism of mystical theology too affective, but the desire to experience the ecstatic dimensions of union with Christ is certainly a biblical ideal.

A Pentecostal Response
Russell P. Spittler

WHO WOULD NOT BE HELPED TO REACH A MIX OF THOUGHT and action that has marked saints from Bernard of Clairvaux to Dag Hammarskjöld, and before and beyond? And surely it is right to locate such piety in nameless grandmothers and unknown Christians in humble places the world around. Not all contemplatives in the church knew themselves to bear the label. A very early one leaned on Jesus' breast.

Are Pentecostals contemplative? Is Pentecostal piety a modern variety of mysticism? I doubt it. You might get that impression from the pose journalistic photographers look for if they want to illustrate a story on the charismatics. Hands raised, head slightly tilted, eyes closed, a woman (usually) shows a pained or rapturous expression. She'll probably have long sleeves and a puritanical neckline, bare of cosmetics and jewelry. All this to perpetuate the myth that Pentecostals are but a shade different from their nineteenth-century holiness forebears. Those who traffic in such stereotypes have their reward.

Whether Pentecostal rapture is a variety of contemplative or mystical experience depends on how the terms are defined. With Dr. Hinson's accurate depiction of classical contemplative piety in the Christian tradition, it hardly serves the truth to think of Pentecostals or charismatics as contemplatives or mystics. If you gave them such labels, they would not readily recognize these new companions.

For one thing, Pentecostals and charismatics do not write devotional literature that speaks of clouds and ladders, dark nights and inward journeys. They would not, being a simple and practical people, make much out of a fascination with God as fire or have much patience with language games that speak of knowing the unknowable.

There is, in the Pentecostal-charismatic tradition, no urge to become one with God, no passion for absorption, little patience for contemplation. Prayer, however, is a different story. Pentecostals pray fervently and fiercely and, some would say, furiously. Over the past few decades speaking in tongues has acquired another name among Pentecostals and charismatics—*prayer language*. This practice, however, may or may not be rapturous. In my lifetime among Pentecostals, I've never known any of them to speak or act as though their glossolalic prayers were contemplative. And glossolalia has not been a characteristic feature of the contemplative or mystical traditions.

While these distinctions exist, related phenomena may mark the Pentecostal at prayer—visions, perceived words of God (at times described as an audible voice) or, to use frequently heard jargon, a heightened sense of the presence of God (or of the the Holy Spirit).

We could, of course, widen and deepen the contemplative tradition by adding into it these Pentecostal phenomena. But I wouldn't suggest doing so. The literature and practices of the contemplative tradition are worthy ones in themselves. There may be along the way a few true contemplatives within the Pentecostal tradition—John Wright Follette and possibly Robert W. Cummings come to mind.

No, let the contemplative tradition flow its own way undiluted by the forced inclusion of glossolalic or visionary Pentecostals. What we are witnessing in this century is rather the birth of a new tradition— one that promises (or threatens, if you prefer) to close the century as Christianity's largest.

CONTRIBUTORS

Donald L. Alexander is professor of biblical theology at Bethel College, St. Paul, Minnesota. Before coming to Bethel, he served ten years as professor of theology and later as dean of graduate studies at the Alliance seminary in Hong Kong. Dr. Alexander has published numerous journal articles in both English and Chinese. *Christian Spirituality* is his first book.

 Sinclair B. Ferguson is professor of theology at Westminster Theological Seminary in Philadelphia, Pennsylvania. A native of Glasgow, Scotland, Dr. Ferguson is a highly respected teacher and author. Among his many publications are *Kingdom Life in a Fallen World, Grow in Grace, Know Your Christian Life* and the *New Dictionary of Theology,* edited with David F. Wright and J. I. Packer.

Gerhard O. Forde is professor of theology at Luther-Northwestern Theological Seminary, St. Paul, Minnesota. Dr. Forde has also taught at Luther College, Iowa, and St. Olaf College, Minnesota. His many publications include *The Law-Gospel Debate, Justification by Faith: A Matter of Life and Death* and *Where God Meets Man: Luther's Down-to-Earth Approach to the Gospel.*

E. Glenn Hinson is professor of church history at the Southern Baptist Theological Seminary in Louisville, Kentucky. He has also taught at Wake Forest University and is a member of the Ecumenical Institute for Spirituality. Among his many publications are *Seekers After Mature Faith, The Integrity of the Church* and *A Serious Call to a Contemplative Lifestyle.*

Russell P. Spittler is professor of New Testament and director of the David J. du Plessis Center for Christian Spirituality at Fuller Theological Seminary in Pasadena, California. Dr. Spittler is a recognized scholar of Pentecostal spirituality. Among his numerous publications are *Perspectives in Neo-Pentecostalism, The Corinthian Correspondence* and *God the Father.*

Laurence W. Wood is professor of theology at Asbury Theological Seminary in Wilmore, Kentucky. Dr. Wood is a noted Wesleyan theologian whose perspective on the Wesleyan doctrine of holiness is also expressed in his book *Pentecostal Grace* and his numerous published articles.